Cornelia Fort

WAFS PILOT

Her Life for Her Country

Cornelia Fort
WAFS PILOT
Her Life for Her Country

by Sarah Byrn Rickman

FLIGHT TO DESTINY PRESS
Colorado Springs, CO

ISBN: 978-1-7350595-3-2
Library of Congress Control Number: 2023901450

Published by Flight to Destiny Press, Colorado Springs, CO 80907

Cover & Interior design by Robert Schram, Bookends Design
Manufactured in the United States of America

Cover caption: In the air flying with a student, flight instructor Cornelia Fort witnessed the Japanese attack on Pearl Harbor on December 7, 1941. She then volunteered to fly military aircraft for the U.S. Army Air Forces and was the third woman to join the Women's Auxiliary Ferrying Squadron (WAFS) and fly for America in World War II. *Courtesy Texas Woman's University Library, the WASP Archives*

Dedication

CORNELIA FORT WAFS PILOT is dedicated to Leontine "Lee" Fort Linton LaPointe, Dudley Fort, Jr., Rob Simbeck, and Judith Miller. These four have given me tremendous support during the development and writing of this book.

Lee (Cornelia's niece) and Dudley (Cornelia's nephew) have helped me tell the most accurate story possible. Lee never knew her Aunt Cornelia but learned the story from her mother, Louise, who was Cornelia's younger sister. Dudley did know his aunt, but he was only seven when she died. Some of his memories are included in this book.

Rob is author of *Daughter of the Air: The Brief Soaring Life of Cornelia Fort*, the first biography of Cornelia, published in 1999. His book was an important source for me when I wrote my first book, *The Originals: The Women's Auxiliary Ferrying Squadron of World War II*, published in 2001. It is the story of the WAFS, the first squadron of women to fly for the U.S. Army Air Forces in World War II. Rob has given me his enthusiastic backing for my young adult-focused biography – the story of Cornelia Fort, the third woman pilot to join the twenty-eight original WAFS.

Judith, cofounder of Redwood Educational Technologies, gave me the incentive to write this book when she sought my input for her new documentary film about Cornelia's life. My book is a companion to Judith's much larger project, *Wings of Courage: The True Story of Cornelia Clark Fort*.

The wings worn by the men and women who flew for the Air Transport Command. *Courtesy Joe Weingarten*

My hope is that Cornelia's story will give today's young women a glimpse of what women pilots had to overcome in 1942 to be allowed to fly military airplanes. To aid their country in wartime, they offered their ability to fly. Deep-seated cultural biases stood in their way, but they did it anyway. I hope Cornelia's story inspires young women to go after what now can be theirs through STEM (the study of science, technology, engineering, and math) and other programs.

Sarah Byrn Rickman, January 8, *2023*

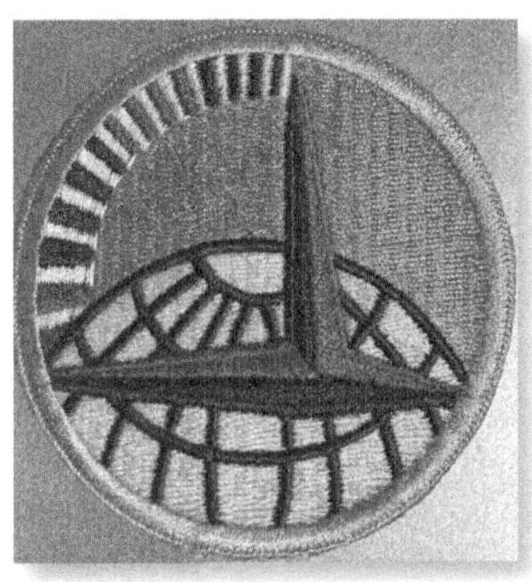

The official patch worn by men and women who flew aircraft for the Ferrying Division/Air Transport Command in World War II. *Author photo*

Contents

Foreword

CORNELIA FORT WAS MY AUNT. As a child, I only learned of her from the memories my mother shared. Cornelia was my mother's older sister by seven years. In 1945, at the age of eighteen, Mother wrote the following brief essay for an English class assignment. Her essay echoes the sentiment she expressed in her recollections. Mother's words best describe Cornelia's admirable character and her exemplary appreciation for the beloved people, places, and things that shaped her brief, purposeful life.

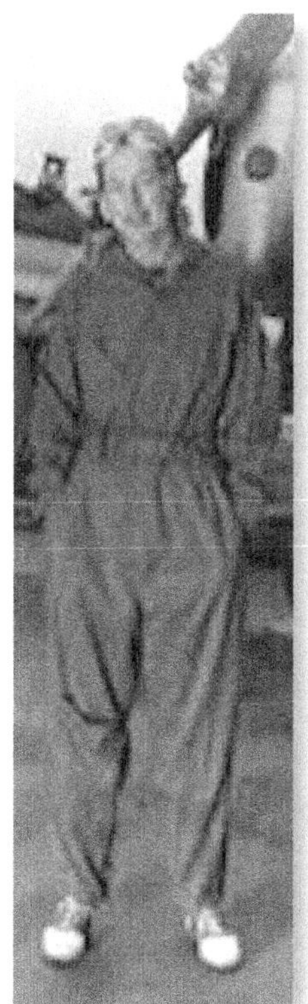

She Loved Life, by Louise Fort

I saw her last as she climbed into the cockpit of her plane and taxied down the runway out of sight. In a few moments the plane circled overhead and dipped its graceful wings in a last farewell. She has gone from this world now, but a day never passes that I do not think of her in many ways. It seems unbelievable that I'll never see her again, for she was so much a part of life.

She loved green pastures and cities, the sunshine on the plains and the rain in the mountains, spring in New York and fog in San Francisco. She loved the ice coldness of the air in the Canadian Laurentians, the good fellows-

Cornelia Clark Fort, Qualified Commercial Pilot and Flight Instructor, 1941. *Courtesy Robert Patterson, grandson of Colonel Robert H. Baker, Commander 2nd Ferrying Group, Wilmington, Delaware, WWII hip in skiing, the peace of sitting in front of a fire, the great dignity of life on the ranches and fox hunting even with its snobbishness. She loved her multitudinous friends and their kindnesses to her. Books and music were deeply personal things to her, "possessions of the soul," as she phrased it.*

She deeply loved the airports little and big, the sky, the planes and yet best of all flying. She loved it best perhaps because it taught her utter self-sufficiency, the ability to remove herself beyond the help of anyone, and in so doing showed her what was of value and what was not. It taught her a way of life, in the spiritual sense. It taught her to cherish dignity and integrity, and to understand more fully the importance of love.

She seemed happiest in the sky at dawn, when the quietness of the air was like a caress, at noon when the sun beat down, and at dusk when the sky was drenched with the fading light. I remember her there and visualize her flying into that clear blue yonder, soaring on through the boundless sky that seems so much a part of her.

Cornelia Fort's story is the sixth such illuminating account Sarah Byrn Rickman has written highlighting the unique set of circumstances that led like-minded individuals to become one of the "Original 28" adventuresome young women pilots to join the Women's Auxiliary Ferrying Squadron between 1942 and 1943.

It is indeed my honor, on behalf of the Fort family, to acknowledge with appreciation the opportunity Sarah is giving the reader to be inspired from learning about our most illustrious relative, Cornelia Fort, and her life-changing path and passion for flying.

Woven throughout the pages are excerpts from Cornelia's heartfelt, well-written letters home to loved ones that will give the reader insight to the thoughtful processing of joyful moments, tragic losses, and professional challenges, which seemingly prepared Cornelia emotionally, mentally, physically, and spiritually to be of great service to her country and a truly honorable, fun-loving human being.

Sarah has told well the story of Cornelia Fort's rebellious, courageous journey. This is an accurate account of how it all happened. Cornelia's coming of age story is still of relevant interest and historically important. There are lessons of value in these pages.

Find how to bravely persevere in the discovery and acceptance of one's unique set of circumstances, interests, aptitudes, and natural talents. Life is all too short and the future uncertain. Savor the moments, seek out and embrace opportunity, find value and meaning in your work, and love life as my Aunt Cornelia surely did.

Leontine Fort Linton LaPointe

Cornelia Fort's portrait photo introduces each chapter: *Courtesy Texas Woman's University Library, the WASP Archives*

Introduction

BE FOREWARNED: THIS STORY WILL BREAK YOUR HEART. The heroine dies in the end, but you already know that. So read on – walk, run, fly with this extraordinary young woman who, during her short life, used her gifts to try to better the world in which she lived.

The story of Cornelia Clark Fort soars. Cornelia herself soared every time she stepped into the cockpit of the aircraft she was flying that day, from takeoff to landing – including her last flight. While doing her sworn duty to the best of her ability, she gave her life for her country when it was at war fighting for democracy and the right to live free. Principles she fervently believed in.

Know that in reading her story you will experience the best of what humanity has to offer. Flying along with this fine young pilot, who died too soon, you will learn what it feels like to dance with birds, chase clouds, and fly the wild blue yonder.

Pearl Harbor, Hawaii, December 7, 1941: Battleship Row on fire. *Courtesy the National Museum of the U.S. Air Force, Dayton, Ohio*

Chapter One

December 7, 1941 — "A Date Which Will Live In Infamy"

MORNING BROKE as it always does in Hawaii, when the big red ball that is the sun rises from the middle of the Pacific Ocean east of the islands.

Cornelia Fort nudged the control stick to the left, touched her foot to the left rudder pedal and put the small, single-engine airplane into a shallow bank. The right wing lifted and traced an invisible arc across the sky as the aircraft, its left wing now pointing down, swung through a 180-degree turn.

The early morning mist had vanished from the green valleys between the rugged mountains that looked down on the calm waters of Pearl Harbor. In the two-plus months she had been here, Cornelia had learned that the seasons in Hawaii did not change like they did in Tennessee. Back home, by early December, the trees on the gentle, rounded Green Hills south of Nashville were bare, and the sky took on that slate gray monochrome that comes in mid-November and stays until March.

Here, in this tropical paradise, the world brimmed with sunshine; gloriously brilliant blossoms of red, purple, orange, and yellow; and smiling people.

She bit back a yawn. Cornelia had been up since before six. Her first student was scheduled to fly at 7:30 this Sunday morning at Honolulu's John Rodgers Airport. It was a busy time. Boys in a hurry to become men were flocking to the airport to learn how to fly. They all had their eyes on the growing threat of a war. All gung-ho to learn how to fly the military's basic training aircraft, which could lead them up the ladder to pilot the U.S. Army Air Forces' faster, more powerful warplanes.

Ernest Suomala, the young man who sat in front of her in the enclosed, two-seat cockpit – one seat in front of the other – was her first student today. They had flown together before. She was finding him to be an apt student.

Cornelia had a full schedule ahead of her that Sunday, as did all the instructors. Most were booked from dawn until dusk. The winter solstice was but two weeks away. Sunset came earlier these days.

Sunday again, Cornelia thought and smiled to herself. Her dear mother would have apoplexy if she knew her darling daughter was flying on a Sunday – very much against the Fort family's strict Episcopal upbringing. But her mother was back home, far across the ocean in distant Tennessee, and Cornelia kept her mother carefully sheltered from the knowledge that her no-longer-little girl was flying on, heaven forbid, Sundays!

When a scan of the sky told her no other airplanes were in the practice area, she tapped her student on the shoulder. "Let's try some power stalls," she yelled over the noise of the engine. "Your airplane," she said, his clue to take the controls.

"I have the airplane," he said, the required response.

Carburetor heat on, power off, stick back, nose up, back pressure, back, back some more. Suomala knew the drill well by now.

Cornelia watched as the nose of the plane climbed higher in the sky, her hands and feet resting lightly on her own set of controls, ready to take over in an instant if the young man failed to perform the maneuver correctly.

There it was, the "mushy" controls, the eerie silence. The little airplane hung, suspended. Then it kicked over to the right.

Suomala did as Cornelia had taught him to do. Stick forward to neutral, power back on, carburetor heat off. All gentle but firm. Back to level flying.

You never could tell with students the first couple of times you took them up. The ones you expected to be bold often turned out to be the most timid once in the air, whereas the poor soul you thought was afraid of his own shadow might turn out to be a roughneck who tended to jerk the plane around all over the sky.

Cornelia, twenty-two, was teaching young men her own age and younger how to fly. And she loved flying the little Interstate Cadet, a high-wing, single-engine trainer aircraft. Like many of the small training airplanes of the day, it was made of heavy cotton fabric stretched taut over an aluminum skeleton of fuselage and wings and painted a distinctive blue and yellow. She thought it the spiffiest airplane around.

"Very nice," she called out when Suomala completed three successful stalls. Then she put him to work negotiating 360-degree turns, first to the right and then to the left, to be accomplished without gaining or losing altitude. "And keep your eye on the altimeter," she reminded him.

Below lay the rainforest – so dense, so verdant, so intense in the early morning sun that it almost hurt to look at it. Lulled by the drone of the engine, mesmerized into a momentary complacency no flight instructor could afford, Cornelia forced herself to look past her student's broad back and beyond the windscreen. She could see the crests of the hills and farther out, the brilliant gem-blue of the Pacific Ocean.

Then in the distance she saw moving specks. What were they?

A flock of birds? Too big. Airplanes? She squinted through the windscreen. The specks – yes, airplanes – and they were coming toward her.

"What's that, Miss Fort?" Suomala asked. He, too, had spotted them.

Now she could make out a formation – dozens of planes. They resembled a swarm of angry bees. Seconds later, the lead aircraft banked right and turned south. She caught sight of a large, red circle on the wings. The other airplanes followed the leader. All but one.

The last plane peeled off and flew toward them. Alarm bells went off in her brain. Her thoughts raced: *The red ball. The Rising Sun? Japanese? Why?*

That sleek, silver airplane was heading right toward them. They were on a collision course, and their much smaller, slower aircraft was the vulnerable one.

"Let's get outta here," she yelled, grabbing the controls from her student.

Cornelia described what happened next in her first-person article published in *Woman's Home Companion* magazine in the summer of 1943.

> *I jerked the controls away from my student and jammed the throttle wide open to pull above the oncoming plane. I remember a distinct feeling of annoyance that he dared disrupt our traffic pattern and violate our safety zone. He passed so close under us that our celluloid windows rattled violently. I looked down to see what kind of plane it was.*
>
> *The painted red balls on the tops of the wings shone brightly in the sun. Honolulu was familiar with the emblem of the Rising Sun on passenger ships, but not on airplanes.*
>
> *I looked quickly at Pearl Harbor, and my spine tingled when I saw billowing black smoke. Might it be some kind of maneuvers? It might be, it must be. For surely, dear God. Then I saw the formations of silver bombers riding in. Something detached itself from a plane and came glistening down. My eyes followed it down . . . down . . . down . . .*

My heart turned over convulsively when the bomb exploded in the middle of the harbor.

Suddenly that little wedge of sky above Hickam Field and Pearl Harbor was the busiest, fullest piece of sky I ever saw. Most people wonder how they would react in a crisis. When the danger comes as suddenly as this did, you don't have time to be frightened. I'm not brave, but I knew the air was not the place for our little baby airplane and I set about landing as quickly as I could.

It was as if the attack was happening in a different time track, with no relation to me. A burst of machine gunfire rattled in my ear. I headed for the runway, landed and taxied the plane toward the hangars. That the attack did have relation to me was brought forcibly to my attention a few seconds later when I saw a shadow pass over me and simultaneously, I saw bullets spattering all around me.

We jumped from the airplane and ran for cover as a second volley of bullets ripped into the tiny plane behind us. We made it safely into the hangar. We counted anxiously as our little civilian planes came flying home to roost. Two never came back. They were washed ashore weeks later on the windward side of the island, bullet riddled. Not a pretty way for the brave little planes and their pilots to go down to death.

Cornelia Fort and her student Suomala survived the December 7, 1941, attack on Pearl Harbor, but some of her fellow pilots who worked at Andrew Flying Service did not. Airport manager Bob Tyce was killed by that last burst of gunfire that Cornelia thought was meant for her.

Could she sleep that night? Did visions of the Japanese plane approaching the little Cadet race through her head – her violent pull up risking a stall and that menacing plane passing underneath, wheeling and firing at her, then accelerating away to rejoin its squadron? What if the pilot hadn't turned away at that moment but had made another pass at her? Surely he would have shot at the defenseless little aircraft. Once hit, they would be headed for certain death. But instead, the pilot turned to rejoin his squadron above Pearl Harbor and the ensuing destruction.

Did another revelation bother her as well? In spite of the horror, the danger, and the glimpse of the pilot in that cockpit who seemed to look straight at her as he dove toward her, all she could remember was the thrill that stabbed her to the core as she looked danger and sudden death in the face for the first time. She had never felt so alive. Now she clung to that feeling as if it were life itself.

In his riveting speech to Congress on the following day, President Franklin D. Roosevelt declared December 7, 1941, "a day that will live in infamy." The U.S. declared war on the Empire of Japan as well as Japan's allies – Adolph Hitler's Nazi Germany and Benito Mussolini's Italy.

Cornelia was one of many Americans stuck in Hawaii. The United States was now involved in a full-scale war. Passage by ship was the best way to get the American civilians home. The port of San Francisco lay well over two thousand miles to the east. And who knew how many Japanese submarines might lie in the deep Pacific waters between them and that all-important destination?

The stranded Americans chaffed under the imposed wait while the politicians and military leaders in Washington, D.C., figured out how to bring them home safely. Our country was now at war, which created all sorts of complications. Would Cornelia ever see her home, Fortland, and those green, Tennessee hills again?

Chapter Two

Did Cornelia Have It All?

SO, WHO WAS THIS GUTSY WOMAN, Cornelia Clark Fort? How did she happen to be in the air over Pearl Harbor on that horrific, historic Sunday morning in December 1941? What is the story behind all this? The answers will take a while to unfold, but it's here. Keep reading!

+++

Cornelia was the fourth of five Fort children. Three boys – Rufus, Jr., Dudley, and Garth – preceded her. Fifth and youngest was her sister Louise.

The Fort family lived in a sprawling, two-story, "old South" mansion named Fortland, which sat on the banks of the Cumberland River east of downtown Nashville. The grand entranceway to the main house sported six imposing, two-story-high columns of the classical Greek Ionic style.

The road leading to the mansion's entryway encircled the fourteen-acre front lawn that daily played host to Fortland's small herd of Jersey milk cows. They grazed there contentedly and undisturbed.

Cows were far from the only livestock at Fortland. The family also owned several horses and a small herd of ponies, along with an everchanging collection of house dogs and barn cats.

Long before Cornelia became enamored with airplanes, horses were her first love. She learned to ride on Fortland's ponies. As she grew older and taller, she moved up to ride the horses in the Fort stable. The groomsman periodically lengthened the stirrups to keep up with her ever-lengthening legs.

She rode every day in the summer, which was sheer joy. The rest of the year she rode as often as possible. When Cornelia got her first pair of blue jeans in the late-1920s, she was hooked. She loved the feel of them, the fit, the style, the "all-purposeness" of them. They were perfect for riding astride. She couldn't understand why she couldn't wear them all the time.

Did she ask, "Why can't I wear my blue jeans into town to get an ice cream cone?"

Was she told, "Nice young girls don't wear trousers in public."

Hardly a satisfactory answer for one so inquisitive, so insistent on knowing why. It made no sense.

"The public? It's just the soda fountain at the drugstore," she probably announced in protest.

It was the 1920s, and she lived in the South where ladies were expected to act like ladies. Already her family was getting used to Cornelia's outspokenness.

When Cornelia began her formal schooling in first grade, she – like her three older brothers – was sent to Ross Elementary School in rural East Nashville, Tennessee. Over the course of several years, Epperson Bond, the Fort family chauffeur, drove her brothers, Cornelia, and her sister Louise to the nearby school.

There, like her brothers before her, Cornelia encountered and learned to get along with people from life's every status and circumstance. Though the Fort family was wealthy, Dr. and Mrs. Fort did not want to raise children ignorant of the many and varied stations in life. The solution: send them to the nearby public school for the early grades.

This decision possibly had a greater impact on Cornelia than her parents had anticipated. The Great Depression hit the United States in the fall of 1929. This devastating event – brought about by the crash of the New York Stock Exchange – caused many people's livelihood to disappear overnight.

Cornelia, now ten years old, was witness to the increasing hardships endured by many of her classmates whose fathers lost their jobs. It was an unexpected and valuable life lesson for her.

By the third grade, Cornelia already was an avid reader. The isolated life she led at Fortland – a good bit younger than her brothers and seven years older than her sister – meant Cornelia lacked playmates her own age. She learned to bury herself in books. Surprisingly aware of the world around her, she missed nothing.

At age twelve, having completed the primary grades, Cornelia advanced to Nashville's well-known and much respected all-girl secondary school, Ward-Belmont. By age twelve, Cornelia had reached her full adult height of 5 feet 10 inches. She towered over all the other girls at Ward-Belmont.

Now Epperson drove Cornelia across town to her new school on Nashville's west side. In the afternoon he picked her up and brought her back to Fortland.

By now Cornelia had become an advanced reader. Epperson noted that, seated in the back seat of the spacious limousine for the long ride across town, her nose remained buried in her current book of choice. She paid no attention to where they were. She didn't care. All that reading was a prelude to something greater, which would begin to unfold as she grew into her teenage years.

Cornelia faced other challenges. Any girl out of "the norm" is in for a rough time growing up.

In the early 1930s, well-bred, young Southern ladies were expected to be reserved and well mannered, certainly not impatient and opinionated. Cornelia was both of these. She knew her own mind. There was a big, fascinating world out there, and she wanted to know all about it.

In those days, girls wore dresses or skirts to school. Some schools, like Ward-Belmont, required girls to wear uniforms.

Pants were only allowed in the gym. When girls reached junior high, they had to don awful-looking blue, green, or yellow bloomer-like gym suits. These were kept – along with a pair of tennis shoes – in smelly lockers next to the gym.

Girls changed into these gym suits to take part in physical education – a forty-five-minute class. They might do a series of exercises. They might play basketball or volleyball – or play field hockey outside when the weather permitted. It varied depending on the season and the gym teacher's schedule on that given day.

Then, hot and sweaty, it was out of the gym suits and sneakers and on to a quick and embarrassing pass through the shower stalls. Stark naked and trying to hide behind a skimpy school-issue towel, the bigger, more developed the girl was, the more to hide and the less helpful the towel.

Daily, Cornelia suffered the indignity of the process.

Back in their skirts and school shoes, the girls returned to their math or English literature classes. This ritual played out at public coeducational institutions as well as private girls-only schools like Ward-Belmont.

Today, girls wear all sorts of pants to school. It's a matter of choice, and it is most certainly allowed.

But what hasn't changed are the feelings so many young girls experience. Deep down inside the agony of not fitting in, of being different, persists. For some, it can overwhelm.

That is what twelve-year-old, five-foot-ten-inch Cornelia dealt with daily. And it was all made worse given the times, social standards, and attitudes. She continued to deal with those feelings, not fitting in, all the way through high school.

So, as you read more here – about Cornelia Fort and some of the gutsy things she does in her teens and in her early adult years – use your imagination. Put yourself in her place.

Sure, being taller and bigger than the other girls when playing field hockey at school should have been an advantage. But in Cornelia's case it made things worse. Cornelia was not athletic. She despised most such activities with the exception of horseback riding.

She towered over all the other girls AND all the boys who attended the occasional school-sponsored, afternoon tea dances and other juvenile mixers that twelve and thirteen-year-olds of both sexes almost uniformly detest.

Finding a dance partner for Cornelia, taller than everyone in the room, was a problem. If there was a shortage of boys, she was forced to dance with another girl. All present had to participate, in other words be out on the dance floor. No wallflowers allowed. If there was an equal number of boys and girls, she often had to suffer the unwelcome indignity of dancing with the shortest boy – an embarrassment to both.

By the time she entered high school, Cornelia dreaded dances.

Betty Rye (Caldwell), her close friend from their Ward-Belmont days, remembering Cornelia's high school years in an interview nearly fifty years later, said, "She had a lot more depth to her than she would show her friends. She thought deeper thoughts than other teens. And she didn't want the boys to know how smart she was."

At twelve, Cornelia was looking at the world through glasses a far different color and tint than her parents – particularly her father. Long before she reached her senior year at Ward-Belmont, her interests with respect to art, culture, and society had turned to the experimental, the modern, the innovative, the decidedly unconventional.

The young, voracious reader was now a budding closet intellectual. And a battle of the wills was brewing at Fortland.

Cornelia's mother was a northerner, a "Yankee" from Boston. Customs, tastes, traditions all across the United States did vary back then – still do to some extent. But Louise Clark, a daughter of privilege and a member of high society in the very refined New England city of Boston, had learned her lessons well.

Already Cornelia had made several extended summer visits to her mother's family in Boston. She became well acquainted with the customs of the North. She liked what she saw. Things seemed less restrictive than in Nashville.

There, Cornelia learned of a new and decidedly different four-year women's college, Sarah Lawrence, located near New York City. She liked what she heard and made it her business to learn more about the school.

Sarah Lawrence College, founded in 1926, was the first liberal arts college in the United States "to incorporate a rigorous approach to the arts with the principles of progressive education, focusing on . . . individual needs."

The college emphasized scholarship, particularly in the humanities, performing arts, and writing and placed a high value on independent study. This was exactly what Cornelia wanted for her college experience. She expressed that interest to her family.

At Sarah Lawrence, students met in small, informal groups with an academic leader who was responsible for their education. The young women were urged to voice their opinions, but they did have to provide supporting evidence for their beliefs either from personal experience or from an authoritative source.

By the end of six months, that leader – referred to as a *don* – would know, beyond a shadow of a doubt, that further examination of certain students was not necessary. Nor were grades. The don already knew the student's grasp of the subject matter – her blind spots, her way of thinking, her ability to put two and two together, and her ability to state her findings convincingly.

Cornelia's father's reaction was extreme and negative. Dr. Fort was familiar with traditional schools that made good use of textbooks, relied on lectures, gave exams, and graded students on their performance.

To Dr. Fort's way of thinking, Sarah Lawrence's approach was next to heresy.

He was convinced Cornelia needed discipline and structure. He was set on sending her to The Ogontz School for Young Ladies near Philadelphia – yes, a northern city. But Ogontz was exactly what Dr. Fort wanted for his headstrong daughter. She needed discipline and purpose in her life. Not only did Ogontz stress those qualities, but it also believed firmly in extensive physical exercise.

Cornelia detested physical exercise.

The school required the young women to participate in military drills. They wore uniforms. They marched. Oh, did they march! Daily! Carrying dummy wooden rifles, they marched up and down the grassy field laid out for their drills, their student leaders barking orders.

Discipline and structure.

Cornelia was not impressed.

She did, however, learn that the famous aviatrix Amelia Earhart had been a student at Ogontz twenty years earlier. Cornelia and every other young woman her age knew about Amelia. She was famous. In 1932, this woman pilot set an aviation record when she flew her red Lockheed Vega on a nonstop, solo flight from North America across the Atlantic Ocean to Northern Ireland. Earhart was the first woman to span the ocean solo and only the second person to do so after Charles Lindbergh.

It turned out that Amelia and Cornelia had much in common. Both became totally enthralled with aviation while in their early twenties. Both were tall. Both were inclined to tomboyishness in their youth. Both were headstrong.

And it was in aviation that both made their mark in history.

+++

Cornelia had her heart set on Sarah Lawrence College. Diligently, she worked toward getting herself there. Through much of her schooling, Cornelia had been rather careless about her academic studies. She had worked hard in the subjects she liked and tended to slack off in those she didn't. Her attitude was not that of a dedicated scholar, and her grades reflected her mindset.

Her initial effort failed. Dr. Fort won the first battle. After finishing her studies at Ward-Belmont, Cornelia – not at all happy about it – was off to Ogontz, the finishing school near Philadelphia. She did not give up.

Previously in the habit of only working on the subjects she liked, at Ogontz she became a totally different student. She worked hard and finished in the top quarter of her class. Partway through her year at Ogontz, Cornelia updated her application to Sarah Lawrence.

Abby Sutherland, the principal of Ogontz, tried to persuade her to remain at the school. She informed Cornelia that if she didn't stay her credits might not transfer to Sarah Lawrence.

Cornelia knew her own mind and stood firm. In addition to overriding her wishes and sending her to Ogontz, that previous summer her father also had denied her the opportunity to travel to Europe with a group of young women she knew and their chaperone. It was 1936, the summer the Olympics were held in Berlin, Germany. Cornelia still smarted under that pronouncement.

Dr. Fort had never been to Europe and saw no reason why his daughter should visit there or even want to. "Stuff and nonsense." Was he possibly swayed by the growing unrest in the "new" Germany under Adolph Hitler?

Cornelia's mother stepped in. Louise Fort advocated that her daughter be allowed to attend the college of her choice. Mrs. Fort strengthened her argument by reminding her husband that though she, herself, had attended Eastern schools for her entire education, it hadn't prevented her, as his wife, from fitting nicely into his Southern way of life and becoming a well-respected matron in Nashville society.

A spoonful of sugar often does help the medicine go down.

Cornelia and her mother prevailed.

In the fall of 1937 Cornelia arrived on the Sarah Lawrence campus – forty-four wooded acres in Yonkers, New York, near the Village of Bronxville – just north of New York City. A thirty-minute train ride from the Bronxville station took students into Midtown Manhattan and all its big-city attractions.

Cornelia's credits from Ogontz, it turned out, did not transfer. There was no explanation of why. Cornelia could have cared less. At Sarah Lawrence, she was a different person and became – to her family's surprise (and maybe chagrin) and to her personal delight – her true self.

Cornelia Fort at twenty. *Courtesy Sarah Lawrence College Archives*

Chapter Three

Escape! Bound for Sarah Lawrence College

CORNELIA FORT WAS ONE of thousands of young women who wanted more from education but were unaware a unique opportunity existed or could not find the path to it. Constance Warren, the president of Sarah Lawrence College from 1929 to 1945, was well aware of this.

Those young women were her inspiration, and she said so in her book, *A New Design for Women's Education*, published in 1940. "The liberal arts college would do well to make its program conform to the changing needs of *youth* in the modern world," she wrote.

Warren was intent on rescuing America's young women from an archaic educational system that gave them little or no substantive education. Beyond the elementary "Three Rs" (readin', 'ritin', and 'rithmatic) learned in grammar school, "education" programs mostly prepared young women to raise children and run a household. Little was intended to stimulate the minds of young women curious about the world beyond their town or city.

Both Cornelia Fort and Constance Warren – kindred souls though two full generations separated them – knew this. They were of like minds, yet they were on two very different life paths.

Warren came into her own by moving in on that male bastion, higher education.

Cornelia didn't know it yet but, like Warren in the field of education, she was in the forefront of a coming shift for young women into new careers where they could make their mark. Cornelia was destined to move into yet another male bastion, aviation – the world of the airplane.

America's establishment was not quite ready for such radical reasoning in the 1930s and 1940s, making Warren and her followers ahead of their time. But young women like Cornelia Fort, already seeking new ideas, were ready to follow.

"Each student, we believe has within herself the seeds of what she is capable of becoming," Warren emphasized. "The purpose of her college education is to enable the student to develop these powers they are born with – to their utmost – and grow into a mature individual, emotionally and intellectually capable of coming to terms with whatever life may have in store for her."

Right there is the personification of Cornelia Clark Fort, age eighteen, as she prepared to enter Sarah Lawrence College in the fall of 1937.

Over her father's objections and with her mother's welcome support, Cornelia got her way. In doing so she opened the door to the life she wanted to explore, experience, and hopefully live.

"Finally, free to follow my own instincts, to take part in, experience, try new ideas, and live each day to its fullest on my terms," she wrote.

Upon arriving at Sarah Lawrence, Cornelia made good on her promise to herself to get involved in activities she thought she would enjoy. Time to take a chance. To get involved. If she didn't like it she could drop out and try something else.

Cornelia gave herself permission.

She immersed herself in the studies she wanted to master. Cornelia was smart, and now she could let it show. Given the academic atmosphere of open discussion in a group setting with their

Cornelia Fort perched on the hood of a friend's car.
Courtesy Sarah Lawrence College Archives

don (leader) she and the other young women shared opinions and a wide variety of ideas, and listened to the responses of others.

The group discussions became Cornelia's tools for learning. She could speak her mind openly. She blossomed.

In the year 2000 the Sarah Lawrence quarterly magazine ran a lengthy article about Cornelia's two years in residence, 1937-1939. Becoming "an academic drudge" – the article said – was not Cornelia's goal at Sarah Lawrence. She enjoyed a good party, and she became fast friends with several women in her dorm: Sarah Lowengart and

Emylu Adams from San Francisco, California; Ann Perdue from Mobile, Alabama; and Rosalie Bangs, from Providence, Rhode Island. An all-American mix.

"All shared backgrounds similar to Cornelia's and their tastes ran to tweed skirts from Brooks Brothers and sweater sets and pearls for everyday wear," the article said. "They began calling her 'Cornie' and – like college girls everywhere – they stayed up late gossiping about men, classes, and the limited opportunities for on-campus social life."

Fond of music, Cornelia took advantage of the close proximity to New York City and its vast musical offerings such as the Metropolitan Opera and the New York Philharmonic. A theater buff, she took in Broadway plays and more avant-garde theater presentations Off-Broadway. New York offered her a potpourri of artistic enjoyment. And then there were the restaurants and museums – excellent food, fun, and culture combined.

Cornelia joined the yearbook staff. She also joined the music club. She studied literature and writing and began to write for *The Campus*, the Sarah Lawrence school newspaper. Her friend Betty Rye back in Nashville already had proclaimed Cornelia to be a superb writer. Proving her friend right, in her second year Cornelia became the Chief Editorial Writer for *The Campus*.

In November 1938, Cornelia put to use her newly discovered awareness and depth of perception. She took notice of a shattering event that happened several thousand miles away on another continent. It was called *Kristallnacht*, the "Night of Broken Glass."

The night of November 9, 1938, a coordinated wave of anti-Semitic violence rocked Germany. *Kristallnacht* refers to the shattered glass – from the windows of synagogues and Jewish-owned stores and homes – that littered the streets of most German towns and cities after Nazi thugs wreaked havoc that infamous night.

The excuse given? It was an unplanned outburst of anger against the Jewish people. But, in truth, Nazi leaders, with German

Chancellor Adolph Hitler's support, planned and coordinated the attack. Also that night, members of Nazi paramilitary groups attacked Jewish communities, burned synagogues, and vandalized Jewish-owned businesses, cemeteries, and homes.

Police and firefighters were told not to protect Jewish homes, businesses, and synagogues. Hundreds of Jews died that night as a result of *Kristallnacht*.

And that was only the beginning.

Stunned when she read the newspaper accounts over the following days, Cornelia started thinking. "What can I do? What can I say?"

She brought up the subject in the daily group discussions. Was the United States aware – really aware – of the horror this represented? Of the evil beneath it all? Of the reality of *Kristallnacht*?

A budding journalist, Cornelia began to think like one. Her job was to write editorials and weren't editorials supposed to clarify things for people and make them think? Cornelia acted. Her editorial on *Kristallnacht* appeared in the November 21, 1938, issue of *The Campus*.

Barbarism a la Hitler

If there is any future left to us in which to record the history of the present, Hitler will be represented as the Dark Man of modern times, a horrible composite of cruelty and criminality.

Five years of barbarism reached its climax last week in Germany. After a five years' "purge", it remained for a minor incident to precipitate a wave of horror unparalleled since the Middle Ages.

Hitler announced his aim, that of purging Germany of all Jews, when he became dictator. How violently and horribly he carried out his aim is all too apparent to everyone able to read the newspapers. . . .

In these five years German Jews have been deprived of even that small quota of freedom left to the rest of the Germans; they have been humiliated and tortured for the simple fact of their Jewish existence. . . .

Last week a young Polish Jew assassinated a minor German official in Paris. With maniacal fury Hitler and his equally rotten hench-men instituted a week of mass cruelty, destruction and horror. With one stroke of the pen Hitler has created a world crisis. He has demolished the last hope of Jewish independence.

A general tax was imposed on all Jews amounting to one fourth of all their property and as the government has records of all wealth, they can set efficiently about their task immediately. After the week of destruction all businesses have been partially wrecked. The Jewish owners must pay for the rehabilitation of their businesses preparatory to handing them over to Aryan ownership at the first of the year.

All Jews have been ejected from universities. They are forbidden to go to the theater, to concerts and to all gatherings at which Aryans will be present. Thus with their business taken from them so is their method of livelihood. That leaves little more than six weeks before all Jews must leave the country.

Other nations of the world have risen to the rescue of the persecuted Jews. Homes must be found for them and money where with to support them until they can stand on their own feet. The Jewish wealth in Germany will remain there because no emigrant is allowed to take more than a few dollars with him out of the country.

But surely this campaign of horror will turn on its creator and smash him also. Surely this wave of barbarism will weaken the ranks of Fascism and restore the faculty of healthy criticism to the mobs blinded with enthusiasm. We should aid the persecuted Jews with one hand and try to hasten retribution with the other.

This, from a nineteen-year-old, privileged American woman. Something was still right in the world.

Chapter Four

"A Coming-Out Party? Seriously?"

CORNELIA, ON A HIGH brought on by the success of her stirring editorial, returned home for Christmas. For nearly a year, Cornelia had known her parents planned to present her to Nashville's high society at her debutante ball – her "coming out" – to be held at the Belle Meade Country Club in late December.

This was *not* something Cornelia wanted.

"I won't do it! It's all a charade!" she had told the family the previous summer when the planning began to gel. Right then, all she wanted was to get back to Sarah Lawrence College and the life she very much enjoyed.

Now, her debut – she considered it an ordeal – was almost at hand. Nevertheless, at her mother's urging, she had bought the ballgown of her dreams in New York in early November. Now she wished she hadn't, because she did *not* want to attend her own coming-out party.

Back home for Christmas, came the confrontation: "You must!" her three older brothers joined their parents in a united front. Not going through with it would hurt the family's name and standing in the community they told her.

A debut is a social gathering with music, dancing, and refreshments. There, a young woman of marriageable age – known as a *debutante* – is formally introduced to society. In Nashville, Tennessee, in the 1930s it was very much part of the social fabric enjoyed by well-to-do families. But it did not fit with Cornelia's new, hard-won concept of herself.

"I will *not!*" she said one final time, but already she was weakening. Deep down she knew how much this meant to her family, how her parents had planned for this occasion. Cornelia loved her parents very much and, in spite of her "new self" discovered and cultivated at Sarah Lawrence, she knew deep down that she must go through with it.

"Oh, all right!"

Cornelia "came out" to Nashville society on December 29, 1938.

"I don't think it was rebellion so much as she hated to be spotlighted," her friend Helen Dixon said many years later. "Cornelia was a realist. She thought it was superficial, and she didn't like ostentation."

True, Cornelia did not like showiness and pretention, but – as it turned out – during that December evening she discovered she very much liked having a really good time. The night of her dreaded debut turned out to be a key turning point in her young life. When the ball was over, Cornelia – in high spirits – invited all her friends to come home with her to Fortland to continue the party into the wee hours.

Those sophisticated outings she had enjoyed in New York City while at Sarah Lawrence definitely had grown on her. Now here she was back in a familiar setting, surrounded by her Nashville friends. Not only did she enjoy the party, she relished it! The revelries lasted until dawn.

In January, Cornelia returned to Sarah Lawrence College for the spring semester.

Cornelia and Sarah Lawrence were made for each other. For a year and a half, she had delighted in finding herself, learning who she was, and learning about the world around her. Cornelia had longed to shed those old hang-ups and mature into a smart, capable young woman who could take the world by storm.

But when she returned to college in January 1939, surprisingly she seemed to lose her way.

During the daily discussion sessions, her don noticed that she was ignoring her studying in favor of more and more socializing. This new behavior in a student he thought was making great strides puzzled him. The maturing process he had noticed throughout the previous spring and fall was now lacking. She was an intelligent young woman with promise, but she appeared, suddenly, to be adrift.

"Until she finds her true direction, her present abilities will not be really fruitful," he noted.

Had the sheer unexpected enjoyment of that night of the coming-out ball truly changed her outlook?

Because Cornelia's Ogontz credits had not successfully transferred to Sarah Lawrence, in the spring of 1939 she had to make a choice. She could take a two-year diploma from Sarah Lawrence that spring and return to Nashville to ponder her future. Or she could return for two more years and complete what promised to be intense and demanding studies. By doing so, she would earn her Bachelor of Arts degree.

Those who knew her well were convinced that's where she was headed. That was the Cornelia they knew.

But Cornelia decided not to return to Sarah Lawrence in the fall of 1939 to continue her education. At the end of the spring term, she returned home to Nashville to stay. Her friends couldn't believe it.

Why? Surely Cornelia valued the vastly important education she would receive by finishing her degree. Yet she was quitting after having achieved, at best, only half of her goal.

Yes, in her two years at Sarah Lawrence she had found freedom of thought. She had become more outgoing. She had begun to take the occasional risk and put herself forward. Now she appeared to turn cautious. Was she doubting herself again?

Did she go home that summer to ponder her future? How close was she to "finding herself"? Who was Cornelia Fort?

Back in Nashville that summer, surprising everyone who knew her, Cornelia joined the Girls' Cotillion Club. Having made their debut, Cornelia and the other "debs" from the previous December were expected to help plan this winter's coming-out ball. Then Cornelia joined the Junior League – another milestone for socially minded young women. Out of the blue, she appeared to be taking on the very role she had so dreaded the previous winter.

Was this an attempt to keep her mother happy? Mrs. Fort had been worried about her independent-minded daughter's future. Now Cornelia appeared to be on the path to fulfilling her "proper" role – marrying well and taking her rightful place in Nashville society.

Nevertheless, her summer of 1939 was not all taken up with social obligations. Once again, Cornelia was free to ride her beloved horses. Her brother, Dudley – equally fond of horses and riding – introduced her to his new passion, fox hunting. Cornelia absolutely loved it! The two spent much of the summer "riding to hounds." Male and female riders, astride their favorite mounts, pursued a wily fox across the green meadows and hills of Davidson County, Tennessee, following a pack of noisy, baying hounds in close pursuit.

In spite of these distractions – pleasurable as they may have been – Cornelia had to decide what she wanted to do with her life. Many avenues were open to her. What, in the long run, proved key to her core values had been revealed in the *Kristallnacht* editorial she wrote in November 1938. But right now, her head seemed in a totally different place.

Then the world turned upside down.

As dawn broke the morning of September 1, 1939, Nazi German military forces invaded Poland. With this act of aggression, World War II began. Britain, France, and others joined the fight in western

Europe. For Americans – for the time being – the reality of war was "over there." But the warning signs of what was to come were obvious to those who paid attention.

✈✈✈

Cornelia's friend Betty Rye had begun dating Jack Caldwell, a friend of Cornelia's brothers Garth and Dudley. Jack was a pilot with the flight school at Berry Field, Nashville's new municipal airport. Cornelia knew Jack as her brothers' friend. But now that he was dating Betty, this put them in the same social circle.

Cornelia heard about Jack's flying and, always curious to learn, queried him about it. "What is it like?" His answers piqued her adventurous spirit. "Come out to the field sometime, and I'll give you a twenty-minute introductory flight," he said.

"Maybe I will," she said.

As fall and winter came on, Cornelia made an even greater effort to adjust and become part of the flow of Nashville society. She was dating. No longer did she try to hide her intellect from the men who now clustered around her. That winter, she was the Tennessee bachelor governor's date when he hosted the Southern Governors' Conference at the gubernatorial mansion in Nashville. In turn, the eligible-bachelor governor attended a holiday dinner party Cornelia hosted at Belle Meade Country Club.

Then 1940 dawned and Cornelia's twenty-first birthday – February 5 – was staring her in the face. Eight months out of Sarah Lawrence, on an excursion through what life in Nashville had to offer, Cornelia had come up empty handed. No clear path or direction. Other than fox hunting, nothing she had tried since returning home had captured her attention, let alone her enthusiasm.

She still had not found herself. Did she, at that point, regret not returning to Sarah Lawrence to pursue that bachelor's degree?

"Now what?" had to be uppermost in her mind.

Chapter Five

Flying? "Cornelia Ate It Up!"

"CORNELIA WANTED to do everything now!"

Jack Caldwell was part owner of Miller Flying Service operating out of Nashville's Berry Field airport. He also was one of the flight instructors. "Cornelia wanted to find out if she'd like flying," Jack recalled. "She decided to take me up on my offer of a twenty-minute introductory flight."

Cornelia had celebrated her twenty-first birthday a month earlier. This introductory flight was her birthday present to herself. She and Jack set a date and time. Cornelia even convinced Betty Rye to ride out to the airport with her. Flying didn't interest Betty, but she thought it would be fun to watch.

When the aircraft, a little yellow Piper J-3 Cub, lifted off the ground that morning, Cornelia knew she had forever left behind life as she knew it. She had entered a new dimension.

Time stood still. She would do anything to capture again – and again, – and again – that rush she felt the moment the wheels left the ground and the little airplane surged upward to become one with the sky. That moment when the aircraft no longer belonged to the earth, no longer was held back by such puny concepts as family allegiances, school, and job – and of course gravity.

Flying symbolized living on the edge. Cornelia liked living on the edge, something that was hard to come by in her sheltered, upper-class, Southern life.

Jack demonstrated simple turns to the left and to the right and how to make the airplane climb and then descend. She begged for more daring stuff. Against his better judgment, he did a stall to demonstrate what the airplane did when it "stopped flying." He did that by pulling the stick back and gradually bringing the nose of the plane up, so it pointed toward the sky. The little plane stopped flying; the engine was quiet. For an instant they hung there in silence. Then the Cub kicked over to the right and, now pointed at the ground, went into a spin.

Cornelia screamed!

Jack wasn't sure if the scream was one of fear or delight.

Effortlessly, he pulled the Cub out of the spin and restored it to straight and level flying.

"Oh, do it again!"

Now he knew the answer. "Cornelia ate it up!"

Jack pulled the nose up into the sky and, once again, the little Cub kicked over into a spin.

There was no scream this time. Rather, what sounded like a rebel yell erupted from the front seat. Jack pulled out and, again, returned the Cub to straight and level flying. The twenty minutes were more than up. "Time to head back," he said.

"I want to fly more, right now!"

Nearly fifty years later, Jack and Betty Rye Caldwell recalled the entire eventful morning in an interview with Rob Simbeck, author of Cornelia's first biography, *Daughter of the Air*.

"I reminded her, an intro flight is twenty minutes," Jack recalled. "I told her, in two hours, you can go back up for a full hour lesson. That still did not make her happy. Cornelia wanted to fly that plane, *right then!*"

Jack landed the plane. Back on the ground, they climbed out of the little Cub. Neither of them spoke. Betty was waiting for them.

"Here came Cornelia, running across the field toward me, her hair flying," Betty said. "She was breathless. She hugged me and announced that she wanted to go 'right back up!'"

Betty had never seen Cornelia's eyes sparkle quite like that. Her face was transformed. Something had happened to Cornelia in the process of that flight and, whatever it was, Betty sensed it might be what her friend had been looking for her entire life.

"Cornelia was determined to go back up for another flight," Jack recalled in that interview all those years later. Finally, she agreed to wait the necessary two hours. Cornelia's mind was made up.

"She was so impatient," Jack said. "If she wanted to do it, she wanted to do it now!"

Teaching Cornelia himself wasn't a good idea. Jack was friends with her brothers Dudley and Garth. He had known her since she was in high school. And now he was dating her best friend. Too many potential conflicts. Besides, Jack had just seen firsthand that if she wanted something and was denied it, Cornelia could be a lot to handle.

"I passed her off to Aubrey Blackburne."

It made good sense. Aubrey was the head flight instructor at Miller Flying Service and had a stellar reputation in the Middle Tennessee flying community. He was steady. He took things slowly, methodically, and thoroughly. That was exactly what Cornelia needed. Having Aubrey, the pro, teach her everything he knew about flying was the best possible solution.

Aubrey and Cornelia clicked. They began with her first one-hour lesson that very afternoon. Slowly and surely, he would take her through the basics of flying.

Initially, she had problems handling the stick, which frustrated her to no end.

"I can't do it," Cornelia said, angry at herself.

"You'll get the hang of it," Aubrey said. "Just give yourself time."

Both the instructor and the student have a control stick. The sticks are attached to the floor of the cockpit and located between each of the pilot's knees. The student uses her right hand to operate the stick. She uses the stick in coordination with the rudder foot pedals to move the airplane left, right, up, down – to do whatever the pilot wants the plane to do.

The student uses her left hand to control the levers and switches, in particular the throttle (fuel and speed control) and the trim knob. (The airplane must be "in trim" to fly straight and remain level.) Cornelia had trouble learning to coordinate the rudder pedals with her feet while manipulating the control stick with her right hand – as do most beginning pilots.

Despite the challenges, Cornelia loved it! All she wanted was to fly again – as soon as she could. And fly she did. As often as possible. Aubrey handled her instruction from that day forward. Slowly, Cornelia's confidence grew, followed by her eventual deft execution of the many various maneuvers.

But all did not go smoothly. Cornelia's flying lessons were barely off the ground when an unexpected tragedy struck the Fort family.

Early in March 1940, about the time Cornelia took that first flight with Jack, Dr. Fort was admitted to Vanderbilt Hospital in Nashville. Over several days his condition steadily worsened. He was still in the hospital two weeks later. His sixty-eighth birthday was March 19, 1940, and the Fort family gathered at his hospital bedside to celebrate the occasion.

Cornelia's father died three days later.

To say the Fort family was turned upside down would be an understatement.

Mrs. Fort knew nothing about her husband's business or his other involvements. She was the loyal, supportive wife, the lady of the house, the mother keeping track of family doings. But without her husband as her anchor, Louise Fort was like a ship adrift. Cornelia, concerned for her mother's wellbeing, insisted that she turn the running of Fortland – a huge, time-consuming task – over to her three sons, Cornelia's brothers.

Through all this, Cornelia continued on her new journey. She had found what she had been searching for since she was a little girl. She was in the midst of self-discovery. Flying became her life. And her father no longer was an impediment to accomplishing what she wanted out of life. She was totally committed to something she dearly loved. Flying made her happy.

Did the fact that real danger was present in flying enter Cornelia's mind? Risk taking was part of the package. Truth be told, the prospect of danger seemed to tantalize her. Aubrey already knew how she attacked learning new, ever-more-challenging maneuvers with an uncommon ferocity.

Cornelia said nothing to her family about her flying lessons. She was twenty-one, free to do as she wished if she had the courage to try. And she did.

Then Dudley, somehow, found out about it. Not surprising. Nashville was a small town at heart, and the aviation community was just beginning to grow. The Fort men didn't fly, but they knew men, like Jack, who did.

Dudley confronted Cornelia soon after Dr. Fort's death: "How dare you fly, knowing our father forbade us to do it?"

Cornelia knew her father had forbidden his sons to fly. She had known since she was five years old. Unnoticed, slightly hidden behind the doorway to Dr. Fort's study, she overheard everything. Her father had brought out the family Bible and made his three sons put their hands on that Bible and swear an oath that they would never fly. Dr. Fort thought flying was a fad, a dangerous and useless one, and he did not want his sons involved. It never occurred to him that his daughter might discover a passion for flying.

Somewhere along the way Cornelia's brothers learned that their sister had overheard that fateful conversation, thus Dudley's accusation.

"Daddy gave that oath to you boys, not me," Cornelia reminded him.

Chapter Six

"Mother, I Soloed Today!"

A MONTH AFTER DR. FORT'S DEATH, Aubrey knew Cornelia was ready for her first solo flight. On April 27, 1940, up she went, alone, in the 50-horsepower, high-wing Luscombe 50 she had begun flying with him.

Two pilots sitting side by side made for better communication between the instructor and a student as intense as Cornelia. Most likely, Aubrey sensed from the beginning that she needed the benefit of that direct communication. So, Cornelia learned to fly in the Luscombe rather than the one-seat-in-front-of-the-other Cub. Up she went on her first solo flight.

She was exultant when she landed. When Cornelia got home late that afternoon, her head was still in the clouds. She had yet to come down, come completely back to earth. All pilots, recalling their first solo flight, understand the magic. They remember how they felt; they know how Cornelia felt.

She went looking for her mother and found her – as she often did – in the garden puttering with her beloved flowers. Barely able to contain herself and her pride in accomplishment, Cornelia blurted out, "Mother, I soloed today!"

Mrs. Fort knew Cornelia was flying. She did not approve. Her rather strange reply that afternoon was: "How very nice dear. Now you won't have to do that again."

Cornelia's worry about her mother deepened that spring. Mrs. Fort was not coming easily out of mourning. Cornelia loved her mother, and she tried, in her own way, to lighten her mother's grief and bring her out of herself. But feeling her own growing self-sufficiency and purpose, Cornelia had her own dragons to slay. She was flying. She loved it. And she was going to keep on flying.

By June she was ready to get her Private pilot's license. All she needed now was one long, cross-country flight – dual – she and her instructor. On June 17, she and Aubrey flew the Luscombe to St. Louis, Missouri, and back – a 600-mile, one-day round trip. He watched her as she carefully checked and precisely followed the map they carried. There was no GPS in those days. In 1940, using a roadmap to find one's way across the sky was a necessary skill for pilots.

Aubrey declared her ready for the big test. But Cornelia wanted one more dual flight. "I want to be good," she told Aubrey. "I want to be thorough. *Being adequate isn't good.*"

It's possible she was trying to overcome some dark self-doubt that she wouldn't admit to anyone – even to herself. Considering Cornelia's struggles with self-doubt growing up, it's understandable. She and Aubrey made one more dual, cross-country flight.

She had logged far more than the fifty hours she needed to qualify for her Private pilot's license. Aubrey signed her off to take her check ride. It was up to her to pass.

Cornelia had to show the flight examiner, a stranger, that she could do more than fly the airplane. She had to prove she was in complete control and could correctly perform all the necessary maneuvers in flight. And she had to show him that – should the engine quit in flight – she knew the procedure to follow to land the airplane safely.

This was a standard check flight maneuver meant to separate those who were truly prepared from those who weren't. In the air, the examiner "pulls the power" (puts the engine on idle) with no warning. The student pilot has to instantly identify a spot to land the plane, be it a farmer's field, a road, or any other flat place.

A real emergency landing can happen anywhere – that's why it's called an emergency. The aircraft, even without power, still has lift and can glide some distance if the pilot keeps the nose down to retain that lift.

But the point in this case is not to actually land the plane, which would be a needless risk since there was no real emergency. Rather, the purpose is to train the fledgling pilot to do two things: One, always to keep her eyes open for a place to land *in case of* an engine failure or other emergency. Two, know what to do to instantly prepare the plane for that emergency landing.

With the power off, the pilot drops the nose of the airplane below the horizon, puts the carburetor heat knob on to avoid a potential fuel blockage, indicates to the instructor where she plans to land, and puts the plane in a gentle glide downward toward her intended landing spot. After the pilot proves she knows what's she's doing, the flight examiner restores the power, and the engine is back on. The student turns the carburetor heat off and returns the aircraft to straight and level flying.

"She came back all smiles," Aubrey said, "with her license in her hand."

She had passed her check ride. Cornelia had earned her Private pilot's license. And she wasn't finished by a long shot.

Author Rob Simbeck notes in his book, *Daughter of the Air*, "Cornelia earned her license more quickly than any Nashville student before her, and she set out to use it."

Cornelia later penned the following recollection:

> *Nothing ever meant so much to me as my private license; it was the first big step up. I took the privileges of that little white*

piece of paper very seriously: "The holder may fly anywhere within the limits of the Continental United States." In the first week I flew well over 2,000 miles. I must admit that lunching in St. Louis, breakfasting in Louisville, flying down to a cocktail party in the Mississippi Delta was very exciting.

+++

After earning her Private pilot's license, Cornelia flew whenever she could. She totaled up hours rapidly. But she soon tired of flights to visit friends in nearby states. She wanted to fly, not play.

Aubrey noted her need to move on to the next level, the secondary phase of flight training. No surprise there. Secondary training required that she fly an aircraft far bigger than the 50-horsepower Luscombe. Next was the big, single-engine, 220-horsepower, open cockpit Waco 7 biplane.

Biplanes have two sets of wings: one set mounted above the cockpit and one below the cockpit. Open cockpit means what it says – the cockpit is wide open to the elements including, of course, the wind and rain. Cornelia was stepping up – way up – to 220-horsepower! One big moose!

The Waco was widely used in the Civilian Pilot Training Program (CPTP). Congress approved "CPT" on August 12, 1939. The initial intent of the program was to encourage civilian flying with the idea of building up the business of aircraft manufacture and its commercial use.

But with the rising threat of war abroad, followed by Germany's 1939 invasion of Poland, CPT became a prime way to train men to become pilots for what then was the very small U.S. Army Air Corps.

By the time Cornelia began flying in 1940, CPT was a going concern. And now, thanks to the insistence of President Roosevelt's wife, First Lady Eleanor Roosevelt and a few other prominent women in Washington, D.C., women could be part of it. Now, one woman was admitted for every ten men selected for the learn-to-fly program. The cost was subsidized by the government, which made it affordable for the average person.

Cornelia loved flying the 220-horsepower Waco. It was in the Waco that she learned to do aerobatics! Cornelia mastered a host of challenging and exhilarating aerial tricks and maneuvers.

Horsing a big airplane like the Waco around the sky was not for the faint of heart, nor was it for one lacking muscle or grit – and probably most important – determination. In those days before hydraulics in aircraft, it took muscle. (Hydraulics operate landing gears, brakes, flaps, thrust reversers, and flight controls of modern-day aircraft.)

Several accomplished women pilots mastered the big plane. It wasn't easy, but Cornelia was determined.

"It was a little tough to do aerobatics," pilot Barbara "BJ" Erickson said of the Waco. Cornelia and BJ would meet two years later and become good friends. BJ, too, had mastered the Waco in order to earn her secondary CPT rating.

"You had to be pretty strong to be able to roll it over and hold it inverted or do a spin," BJ said. "Normally an airplane doesn't take strength to fly. Usually it's fingertip control, but this one took muscle."

With Aubrey's patient instruction, Cornelia too mastered the Waco and the art of aerobatic flying. Ultimately, she excelled at it, learning, step by necessary step, how to tackle challenging maneuvers while hanging upside down in the open cockpit with only her harness holding her in.

She learned about spins and how to recover from them. She learned everything that Aubrey had the ability and patience to teach her, which was exactly what she wanted and needed. Even more telling, she absorbed the confidence he strove to instill in her. Confidence became Cornelia's newly found weapon.

Cornelia earned her commercial license on February 8, 1941, three days after her twenty-second birthday. A few weeks later she added her instructor's rating.

In one year's time, Cornelia Fort had evolved from willful flight student and fledgling pilot into a steady, accomplished, commercial pilot who was also qualified as an instructor for other fledgling, wannabe pilots.

CPT was designed to encourage and financially assist college-age men and women who wanted to learn to fly. Could Cornelia possibly get a job where she could use her newly acquired instructor's rating to teach fledgling military pilots?

In that interview with Rob Simbeck all those years later, Jack Caldwell pointed out – with some degree of pride in his voice because he had set everything in motion – that "Aubrey took Cornelia all the way to her commercial license by early 1941."

Aubrey stayed with Cornelia until she accomplished what she so devotedly set out to do.

"Flying apparently added a sense of wonder and joy to her life," her sister Louise later said. "Hers had been a lumbersome, cumbersome growing up. Many of our Nashville friends were meadow mousey, and we had lived in a very traditional style.

"I think she was a great rebel of her time."

Chapter Seven

"Mister Cornelia Fort, Come Fly for Us"

WITH HER COMMERCIAL LICENSE and instructor's rating under her belt, Cornelia wanted to broaden her experience. Teaching an occasional student in Nashville wasn't enough. Hoping to land a job as a flight instructor, she wrote to nearly every flight school in the country. She even wrote to one in Honolulu, Hawaii.

She hit paydirt! A new flight school in Colorado was looking for instructors. In June 1941, the following telegram arrived at Fortland. It was from Massey-Ransom Flying Service, Inc., in Fort Collins, Colorado:

"MR. CORNELIA FORT. YOU ARE ACCEPTED AS A FLIGHT INSTRUCTOR. REPORT AT ONCE."

Shaken by the "Mr." – they had assumed Cornelia was a man – Cornelia, tears flowing, showed the telegram to her mother. "They think I'm a man!" she wailed. "I can't go!"

Louise Fort rose to the occasion. She called Epperson and asked him to drive them to the local telegraph office. With her mother directing her reply, Cornelia sent a telegram to Fort Collins, explaining that she was *not* a mister, but a miss.

The immediate reply:

"MR. OR MISS OR MRS. FORT. WE DO NOT CARE WHAT YOU ARE IF YOU CAN TEACH FLYING. REPORT AT ONCE."

Hurriedly, Cornelia packed for the trip. Her plan was to drive her car cross country to Colorado with her Irish setter, Kevin, as her companion. This, however, was too much for her mother, who was horrified by such an unconventional idea.

"Cornelia, dearest, no genteel woman, particularly one only twenty-two years old, should drive halfway across the United States by herself!"

The compromise: Epperson drove Cornelia to Fort Collins in her car. After he deposited her safely at her destination, he took a Greyhound bus back to Nashville.

Cornelia and her new students – flying a Luscombe – began logging hours over Larimer County, east of the foothills of the magnificent Rocky Mountains. From Fort Collins one has a view, to the west, of one of Colorado's most majestic mountains: Longs Peak, elevation 14,256 feet.

She logged hours very quickly, as Massey-Ransom was a busy place. Then with considerable instructing hours under her belt, Cornelia took a few days off.

She had been invited to attend her Sarah Lawrence friend Ann Perdue's wedding. She took off for Mobile, Alabama, and what proved to be a joyous reunion for the five young women who had been so close in 1938 and 1939.

On her return to Fort Collins, when not flight instructing, Cornelia began writing the following article. In it she vividly described her flying life. When she was satisfied with it, she sent it to Sarah Lawrence, hoping her alma mater would publish it. And they did.

The *Alumnae Magazine* ran Cornelia's article in the October 1941 issue.

Lady-Bird

"How did you start flying?"

If only I had some answer, any answer to that question, but I don't. Frankly, I don't even remember.

I shudder when I think how easily I might have missed that road that led to the airplanes, the misty summer sunrises and the aching profitless hours of practice with the sun beating down – and to all the little remembered bits of happiness that fit into the flying pattern.

Let me start with the too common notion that flying is glamourous. Too many girls have entered aviation with only a desire for shining white coveralls, a helmet, goggles, and the "fine free wind" in their hair. These sorry sisters have caused the rest of us to have to fight hard for even an ounce of recognition and respect we have earned.

Flying isn't glamourous or even adventurous in the ordinary sense of the word. It is heart-breaking, back-breaking work. The adventures we all have that make such wonderful stories afterwards seem, at the time, only desperate moments when we were completely helpless. Moments for which we would gladly turn in our flying suits to have done without.

You ask me why we fly?

"For room and board" is the only logical answer. Further explanations are vague, because we cannot manage to put into words what it is that really keeps us at it. The only answer is the trite phrase "it gets under your skin – deep down inside."

The question I am asked most often is whether my students (all boys) resent a female instructor. Strangely enough they don't seem to. I think the explanation is in the psychological set-up. They are so completely helpless at first. After leading them by the hand for eight hours up to the climax of soloing,

I have made them so dependent upon me that they seldom think of me as anything other than the instructor.

I still remember my first lesson vividly – my instructor turning the plane over to me at the safe altitude of 2,000 feet and telling me to keep it level with the stick. I had a terrible time, and finally turned to him in desperation. He was most amused. "Soon," he chuckled, "you won't even think about the plane's being level. You will feel it as automatically as you drive a car."

We earthbound creatures are so used to having a constant reference point, the ground, that we can't realize what it means to be without it, as one is in fog, which wraps the plane in a thick blanket, completely destroying one's sense of equilibrium. This situation is so serious that there is a law to cover it: if the pilot is at any time unable to see the ground for more than 3 minutes at a time she must immediately go on instruments, return to base or immediately set down.

When I got my commercial license I thought that I would be satisfied, but this flying is like an awful thirst; one wants to learn more and more and to accumulate ratings. The more experience I get the less I seem to know, which is terribly discouraging.

I came out here to Fort Collins, Colorado, to get altitude experience – the hardest flying there is. We are a mile high (5,280 feet) here, which is higher than most light plane pilots ever get at sea level. I'm flying off the side of the Rocky Mountains where the air is tricky and vicious, and one learns plenty and fast.

All of us have the wanderlust. We either fly because we have it or acquire it because we fly. I believe, too, that flying is a character-builder; there is absolutely no one to rely on, no help, no advice, no comfort. One's decisions and the skill that flows out of one's hands are the only realities. And that alone-

ness, which is so really terrifying at first, becomes eventually something useful and free and warmly good.

In the meantime, Cornelia had earned her ground instructor's certificate and now began teaching ground school for students as well as doing in-the-air flight training. This gave her yet another certification to add to her teaching portfolio.

She found time to hop back in a Waco to practice her slow rolls, roll-off-the-top Immelmann turns, and loops – all aerobatic maneuvers.

Then – out of the blue – came the opportunity of a lifetime.

Cornelia received a letter all the way from Hawaii. It was a much belated response to her job-hunting inquiries from the previous spring. Andrew Flying Service, operating out of John Rodgers Airport in Honolulu, was looking for flight instructors. They offered her a job! It paid very well! She wanted it!

She turned in her notice and prepared to move to the U.S. territory of Hawaii.

One of her Ft. Collins students wrote this note to her, but Cornelia did not receive his letter until a year and a half later. Her mother had to forward it to her. And it was unsigned. Nevertheless, she cherished it. In part, it reads:

My first "ride" when we flew to Greeley for the "chutes." Your laughter the first time we "spun." The moonlight on the highway when we drove home from the rodeo. Your tears and kiss when I soloed. Please don't mistake this for a romantic love note. It is the note of a youth inspired and awed by a marvelous woman. I enjoyed those days and you more than you could ever know.

On September 20, 1941, she boarded the steamship *Mariposa*, Honolulu bound.

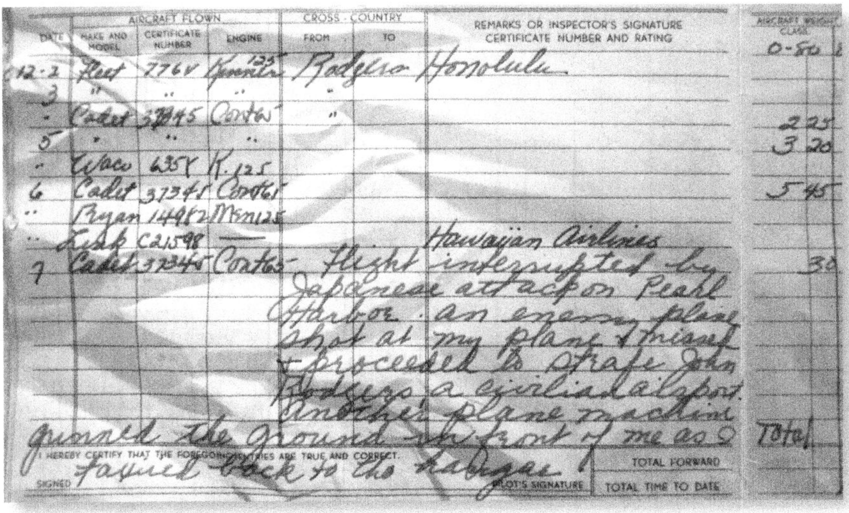

DATE	AIRCRAFT FLOWN: MAKE AND MODEL	CERTIFICATE NUMBER	ENGINE	CROSS - COUNTRY: FROM	TO	REMARKS OR INSPECTOR'S SIGNATURE CERTIFICATE NUMBER AND RATING	AIRCRAFT WEIGHT CLASS 0-80
12-2	Fleet	776V	Kinner 125	Rodgers	Honolulu		
3	"	"	"	"			
"	Cadet	37345	Cont 65	"			2 25
5	"	"	"				3 20
"	Waco	635V	K. 125				
6	Cadet	37345	Cont 65				5 45
"	Ryan	14982	Men 125				
"	Fisk	C21598	—			Hawaiian Airlines	
7	Cadet	37345	Cont 65			flight interrupted by Japanese attack on Pearl Harbor. an enemy plane shot at my plane & missed & proceeded to strafe John Rodgers a civilian airport. Another plane machine	30

gunned the ground in front of me as I taxied back to the hangars!

I HEREBY CERTIFY THAT THE FOREGOING ENTRIES ARE TRUE AND CORRECT.

SIGNED — PILOT'S SIGNATURE

TOTAL FORWARD — Total

TOTAL TIME TO DATE

This page from Cornelia's log book contains flight lessons given on December 2, 3, 5, and 6 leading up to and including the fateful flight on December 7, 1941, when the Japanese attacked Pearl Harbor and an enemy aircraft shot at her and her student Suomala. She gives her own description of the attack and their escape. *Christopher Miller/Redwood Educational Technologies/WASP Archives, Texas Woman's University Collection.*

Chapter Eight

From Paradise to Hell in Two Hours

ON THE MORNING OF SEPTEMBER 29, 1941, Cornelia recorded her first flight out of Honolulu's John Rodgers Airport. It was a familiarization flight. She had to learn the geography of this new place – Pearl Harbor and the adjacent city and environs of Honolulu – over which she would be flying with students.

That afternoon she went to work. Cornelia logged three hours and five minutes instructing in Interstate Cadet 37345, followed by forty minutes in a Taylorcraft. The following day, September 30, she flew students in a Piper Cub, then again in Cadet 37345, followed by flights in a Fleet and a Ryan ST – all trainers. Over time, she would record many instructing flights in the little blue and yellow Cadet with the tail number 37345.

By October 1, she was getting her feet wet. In addition to flying with students in the trainers, she also got in a flight in a Waco. Cornelia had to be smiling after that! The following days found her in the Waco again. Obviously, at least one of her students was advanced enough for flying lessons in the "big plane."

On October 3, she wrote to her brother Dudley that she had found an apartment in Waikiki. She thanked him for his two letters, which had caught up with her at her various stops enroute to

Hawaii. Very pointedly she commented on his remark: he hoped she was "going to church while away from home."

Her answer:

For six months I worked all but two Sundays and those two I slept in. Don't worry about my soul – I realize how wonderful our childhood was, how lucky beyond hope of written word we are to have had such parents.

Then on a different note: *This is an excellent place to work. A good organization and good planes. I'm flying more open ships – stunting biplanes like the Waco – than I've ever flown before. It's all a lot of fun.*

Over the next two months, Cornelia flew daily, teaching a lot of young men to fly. She relished every minute of it.

On November 14, she wrote this surprisingly introspective letter to her oldest brother.

Dear Rufus,

As you probably gathered from my letters to Mother, I'm of two minds about Honolulu – it is truly beautiful and such weather as could never be found anywhere – all blue and green and gold – sunshine without that drenching heat you might expect in the semi-tropics. I spend my one day off prone on the beach (and not Waikiki, that Coney Island of the Pacific) absorbing sun and surf and resting up from my soldier-sailor-defense worker students. This is really a boom town, and that I don't like. Hectic and full of petty and not so petty irritations.

I'm glad I came, but the islands are not for me. I miss the season changes and the trains that take you places. There is a Toonerville Trolley Train that putters around the island. One of the local proverbs says that when that train begins to look like a train on the mainland, it's time to go home. Already it looks bigger, bigger to me, and last midnight I heard it whistle. That peeping little whistle contained all the magic of unknown places.

If ever you have read Thomas Wolfe's books and his descriptions of trains and that quality of wonder contained in a smoky line of cars hitched together on the rails, you may understand what I mean.

There's so much poetry in so many things, my dearest. I've had so much happiness given me and for all of it I am grateful to everyone who has touched my life and added joy. And so many times a day I'm choked with love and gratitude to Mother and Dad, who made my way of life possible and who gave us our standards of integrity and loyalty and the ability to love life and value wisdom and beauty.

The happiness I have earned for myself is deeply good, too. The friends I've known in so many places, the knowledge I've thirsted for and gained, and the limitless prospect of more and more, the simple fact of having earned a living for myself with my hands and the skill that they can produce, the deeply satisfying pleasure of flying and the convictions such as they are that I have come to.

And if I leave here I will leave the best job that I can have (unless the national emergency creates a still better one), a very pleasant atmosphere, a good salary, but far the best of all are the planes I fly. Big and fast and better suited for advanced flying.

By December 2, Cornelia had been in Honolulu just over two months, and she had logged sufficient instructing and flight hours to raise her grand total of hours flown to a most impressive 878:05.

Though she had been flying for less than two years, Cornelia was one very experienced young woman with many hours in the cockpit.

Five days later, Cornelia and the Cadet with tail number 37345 once again flew the skies over Pearl Harbor. That day, she and that little aircraft made history. It was December 7, 1941 – "a date," President Roosevelt later declared, "which will live in infamy."

That day, war came to Hawaii and to the United States of America.

+++

At first while living in Waikiki, Cornelia stayed somewhat to herself. But soon after her arrival, she met Betty Guild whose family lived in Honolulu. Betty and Cornelia had similar backgrounds. Without her family knowing about it, Betty had learned to fly at age fifteen. Now twenty, she had earned her limited commercial license, the first step toward the kind of certification Cornelia now sported.

Betty, with aspiration to one day be a flight instructor, worked for Andrew Flying Service, sending out billing statements and handling paperwork. That put her at the John Rodgers Airport almost daily. When she and Cornelia met, a friendship was born.

Cornelia also met Bill McCain, a Navy lieutenant and one of her first flight students. Like Cornelia, he tended to be intellectually inclined. He gravitated to books and small gatherings rather than to raucous parties and a crowded social scene. She had found a kindred soul. He, however, fell head over heels in love with her.

Cornelia liked Bill, but she did not share his passion. Eventually this relationship would create conflict between Cornelia and her mother. Mrs. Fort, for whatever her reasons, did not approve of Bill's courtship of her daughter. It was never clear why. Bill, well educated, was from a good family and had excellent prospects. Nevertheless. . . .

After the Japanese attack, life in the Honolulu area changed drastically.

The attack on Pearl Harbor crippled the U.S. Pacific Fleet. More than 2,000 military personnel were killed including some of Cornelia's friends and students.

On December 8, Cornelia called Betty, and they toured John Rodgers Airport to look over the damage. Cadet 37345, that little blue and yellow plane Cornelia and Suomala had abandoned on the runway when they escaped into the hangar, was riddled with bullet holes.

Immediately after the bombing of Pearl Harbor, all nonmilitary air traffic on the Hawaiian Islands was shut down including all student-instruction flights out of John Rodgers Airport. There was no more flying for Cornelia or Betty or any civilian in Hawaii for the rest of the war.

Cornelia found a job taking applications for work supervised by the U.S. Army engineers. She moved in with the Andrew family. Since there was little else to do in wartime Hawaii, she spent evenings and weekends reading and writing letters. In January 1942, she wrote this thought-filled letter to her mother. It reads like an epitaph.

> *My life has been rich and full of meaning. I've loved the green pastures and the cities, the sunshine on the plains and the rain in the mountains. Springtime in New York and fog in San Francisco.*
>
> *Books and music have been deeply personal things to me, possessions of the soul. I've loved the multitudinous friends in many places and their many kindnesses to me. I've loved the steak and red wine and dancing in smoky nightclubs, self-important headwaiters who bring reams of French bread and wine sauces in New Orleans. I've loved the ice coldness of the air in the Canadian Laurentians, the camaraderie of skiing and the first scotch and soda as you sit in front of the fire.*

I loved my blue jeans and the great dignity of life on the ranches. I loved fox hunting even with its snobbishness, I loved the deep pervading tiredness after six hours of timber-hopping.

I dearly loved the airports, little and big. I loved the sky and the planes and yet, best of all, I loved flying. I loved it best perhaps because it taught me utter self-sufficiency, the ability to remove oneself beyond the keep of anyone at all – and in so doing it taught me what was of value and what was not.

It taught me a way of life – in the spiritual sense. It taught me to cherish dignity and integrity and to understand the importance of love and laughter. . . .

If I die violently, who can say it was "before my time"? I should have dearly loved to have had a husband and children. My talents in that line would have been pretty good but if that was not to be, I want no one to grieve for me.

I was happiest in the sky – at dawn when the quietness of the air was like a caress, when the noon sun beat down and at dusk when the sky was drenched with the fading light. Think of me there and remember me, I hope as I shall you, with love.

Cornelia had nearly 900 flying hours in her logbook, but now she was grounded! She wanted to get out of Hawaii. She wanted to go home to the United States, to Nashville, wherever she could do "something more constructive for my country than knitting socks!" But the government had put a ban on anyone leaving the islands.

Finally, her passage to The States was booked as part of a convoy of civilian and military vessels leaving Honolulu in late February 1942. Knowing her ocean passage would be risky and subject to attack, a month before sailing Cornelia wrote to her mother:

I'm filled neither with a feeling of morbidity nor a prescience of disaster. But the ocean voyage I will be making shortly has elements of danger, and if I lose my life before seeing you again, dearest, I wanted to say "aloha" and send you my love forever and forever.

Just in case, she drafted her will and testament and included it with the letter to her mother. She specified two gifts. Indicative of who Cornelia had become, she wished to leave enough money to Sarah Lawrence College to fund several scholarships for young women from the Southern states – women who could not otherwise afford such a school. She believed so firmly in the goals of her alma mater that she wanted other deserving young women to have the same opportunity she had. The second asked that her beloved dog, Kevin, be well taken care of.

At some point later on, Cornelia wrote the following note to a friend regarding her growing appreciation of Hawaii:

> *I had the world's best job and loved it violently and could have had it until I died of old age had not the Japanese come calling. . . . The weather was ideal, the students pleasant, the planes wonderful, the pay exorbitant, the hours delightful. And when work was done there were so many places to play and so many nice people to take me playing. All in all, coupled with the music and flowers, I was exceedingly pleased with life.*

Cornelia – at the studios of WSM Radio – prepares to speak to her Nashville audience about the attack on Pearl Harbor. *Courtesy Sarah Lawrence College Archives*

Chapter Nine

Pearl Harbor Survivor Is a Hometown Celebrity

ON MARCH 1, 1942, the ship bringing Cornelia and the others home steamed under the Golden Gate Bridge into the Port of San Francisco. She planned to spend a few days there with friends, noting in a letter: "Had a fun reunion with Sarah Lawrence pals Sally Lowengart and Emylu Adams!"

Her status as a celebrity – a woman pilot who survived the attack on Pearl Harbor – preceded her back to the mainland. An Associated Press reporter and photographer tracked her down for an interview. The reporter wrote: "Miss Fort wants more flying, preferably ferrying planes for the Army."

She had arranged to have her car shipped to her from Nashville. Cornelia planned a leisurely cross-country drive back to Tennessee, stopping to visit friends as well as sightsee along the way. This time her mother didn't try to stop her.

Cornelia missed flying in the worst way! She had been grounded for more than ten long, dull weeks. She was aware that all nonmilitary flying was shut down within 100 miles of America's coastlines. To her great relief, she discovered that some civilian flying was permitted inland. She held instructor and commercial ratings. She could continue to fly.

Her logbook notes: "March 12, Tucson, Arizona. Rented a Fairchild 19 primary trainer and took a thirty-minute spin around the area." From that vantage point, she could look down on the vast desert filled with saguaro cactus and an assortment of other prickly plants and desert-dwelling animals.

The next flight to show up in her logbook is on March 22 in Nashville – back at Miller Flying Service. Cornelia treated herself to an hour of aerobatics in the Waco. Then, just for fun, she rented a J-3 Cub and took it up for another half hour.

Flights to Muscle Shoals, Alabama, and to Chattanooga, Tennessee – likely visits to friends – show up in her logbook later in March. All her April flights are local and nearly all are in a J-3 Cub. Most are short flights, a little less than an hour. She was "staying current," a necessity for a flight instructor and for any active pilot.

Back home in Nashville, Cornelia – now *the* local heroine, a bona fide survivor of Pearl Harbor – was called on for newspaper and radio interviews and to speak at all sorts of functions, from selling U.S. War Bonds to addressing the local Civil Air Patrol meeting.

Cornelia – dressed in an immaculate suit and high heels and wearing both a lei from Hawaii and her prized pearls – stands proudly in front of a microphone at the studios of WSM Radio in Nashville. She is surrounded by staff, technicians, and all the paraphernalia of a radio broadcast in 1942. She spoke to her Nashville audience about that infamous day in December 1941.

Like most Americans, Cornelia wanted to get even for the attack on Pearl Harbor and to avenge the people, both military and civilian, who had died there including several who were her friends and students. While still in Honolulu, she wrote:

> *Each of us had some individual score to settle with the Japanese who had brought murder and destruction to our islands.*

By summer, her celebrity status began to wear thin and boredom threatened to drive her crazy. She contacted the U.S. military to volunteer. But the military – though in desperate need of pilots – was not interested in putting women pilots to work.

Then a ray of hope appeared. She could become part of the first all-female Link Trainer Operator Class at Link Headquarters in Binghamton, New York. The Link Trainer, also known as the "Blue Box" or "Pilot Trainer," was a stationary flight simulator produced between the early 1930s and early 1950s. During World War II, it became the key pilot training aid used by almost every combatant nation.

The U.S. Army needed more instructors, so the military began hiring women to teach instrument flying in the Link. Cornelia was accepted and told to report to Binghamton.

Driving north from Nashville, Cornelia planned to make two stops. First she spent the night with her Nashville friends Betty and Jack Caldwell, now living near New York City. Jack was flying for the Air Transport Command (ATC), part of the U.S. Army Air Forces.

Having introduced her to flying, Jack was particularly pleased to hear of her plans. He told her it was the best possible option for her to master this war-related skill. It would lead to a job teaching budding military pilots to fly on instruments – a proficiency they had to have.

Cornelia made it clear that, for her, this was a stopgap measure. What she really wanted was to fly for her country in time of war, not instruct others.

"Cornelia, the likelihood of you flying with the military just isn't going to happen," Jack told her. He cautioned her not to throw away the potential future opportunities the Link job could give her.

From there, she headed to Locust Valley on Long Island, New York. Cornelia had continued to correspond with Bill, the Navy lieutenant who had fallen in love with her in Hawaii. His parents had a summer home on Long Island, and they had invited her for dinner and to spend the night before she traveled across the state to Binghamton. They were delighted to meet her, and Cornelia liked them very much.

The next day, she was on her way to Binghamton.

There, she embarked on her new career, teaching Link instrument flying to male students bound for the U.S. Army Air Forces or Naval Air Force. Life wasn't going too badly. But she wasn't flying.

+++

Two and a half months later, out of the blue, came yet another miracle!

Cornelia received a telegram from the Air Transport Command, United States Army Air Forces. It was dated September 5, 1942, and signed "Love" and "Baker." Cornelia would soon learn that "Love" was Nancy Harkness Love, a fellow woman pilot. "Baker" was Colonel Robert H. Baker, newly appointed Commander of New Castle Army Air Base, Wilmington, Delaware.

The telegram read: "ADVISE IF YOU ARE IMMEDIATELY AVAILABLE TO JOIN A GROUP OF WOMEN PILOTS UNDER THE AIR TRANSPORT COMMAND TO PERFORM DOMESTIC FERRYING DUTIES."

Cornelia wired her mother in Nashville: "THE HEAVENS HAVE OPENED UP AND RAINED BLESSINGS ON ME. THE ARMY HAS DECIDED TO LET WOMEN FERRY SHIPS AND I'M GOING TO BE ONE OF THEM."

Cornelia Fort was one of eighty-three experienced women pilots selected to receive that telegram.

+++

Before Pearl Harbor and the declaration of war on December 8, 1941, many U.S. military pilots were "on loan" to the Ferrying Division, the major unit of the Air Transport Command. Those pilots had been borrowed from their permanent jobs to perform another critical job: they were needed to ferry (move) new airplanes from the factories building them to recently established Army and Navy flight training schools.

Immediately after Pearl Harbor, all those pilots were called back to their regular units.

As the U.S. geared up to fight this unanticipated war, production of new training planes skyrocketed. Aircraft rolled off assembly lines in ever-increasing numbers. But now, there were no pilots available to fly them to the flight training bases where, already, young Army Air Forces recruits were lining up to learn to fly.

Colonel William H. Tunner, in command of the Ferrying Division, Air Transport Command, U.S. Army Air Forces, was responsible for moving those planes. He was faced with rebuilding his ferrying operation from scratch. He was, in his own words, "combing the woods for pilots."

Most men qualified to fly military planes – and who weren't already in the service – were working as certified civilian flight instructors. The key word here is *men*.

The idea of using experienced women pilots to ferry military airplanes had surfaced in 1940. But the old guard military men, saddled with a "good ol' boy" mentality, envisioned no such notion. The Army brass rejected it to a man. Need was completely ignored. They didn't understand women, and they most certainly did not want to deal with them.

Using women to ferry aircraft was not Colonel Tunner's idea either, but then fate dropped a well-known woman pilot by the name of Nancy Harkness Love into his midst. Colonel Tunner heard her out. She knew of nearly 100 women pilots who were qualified to ferry the 165-horsepower training aircraft he was desperate to move.

Colonel Tunner made up his mind and made a difference – not only to the war effort but to the future of women pilots in the military and in aviation in general. He asked Nancy Love to come to work for him and to recruit those qualified women pilots.

Finally, the opportunity for women to fly for the U.S. military was at hand.

Nancy Love, age twenty-eight, was named director of the squadron organized under the Ferrying Division of the ATC/USAAF. They would be known as the Women's Auxiliary Ferrying Squadron (WAFS). The women, however, remained civilians.

Already, Colonel Tunner knew where he wanted his WAFS pilots based: New Castle Army Air Base, Wilmington, Delaware. The PT-19 single-engine, 165-horsepower, primary trainers he needed to train fledgling military pilots were, at this moment, rolling off the assembly lines at Fairchild Aviation in nearby Hagerstown, Maryland.

In addition, Piper Aircraft Company, located in nearby Lock Haven, Pennsylvania, was turning out small Army liaison aircraft that also needed to be ferried to locations around the country. His women ferry pilots could ferry those planes as well as the PT-19s.

Colonel Tunner moved forward.

Colonel Robert H. Baker, the newly appointed commander of New Castle Army Air Base, and Nancy Love already were well acquainted. Nancy and her husband, Bob, ran a flight service for which she ferried many an airplane. When Bob Love, an Army Reservist, was called up after Pearl Harbor, they closed down their flight service operation in Boston, and Nancy moved to Washington, D.C., with him.

Nancy, well versed in the business of ferrying airplanes, immediately went to work for Baker at the Ferrying Division's Baltimore location in spring 1942. Now, for Colonel Tunner, these two, together, would make this WAFS squadron at New Castle Army Air Base work like clockwork.

Nancy Love now carefully selected women she recognized as qualified for this revolutionary idea – recruit highly experienced women pilots to support the war effort by ferrying trainer planes.

On September 5, 1942, she and Colonel Baker sent telegrams to eighty-three American women, ages twenty-one to thirty-five. All were known to have logged at least 500 hours in the air, to hold commercial licenses as well as 200-horsepower engine ratings, and to have recent cross-country flying experience.

Thanks to her outstanding flying credentials, Cornelia Fort was one of them. Her new employer was the Ferrying Division, Air Transport Command.

Nancy Love welcomes Cornelia Fort, Helen Mary Clark, Aline "Pat" Rhonie, and Betty Gillies, the first four to arrive. *Courtesy Sarah Lawrence College Archives*

Chapter Ten

Cornelia the Second to Report

FIRST TO ARRIVE at New Castle Army Air Base in Wilmington, Delaware, was Betty Huyler Gillies – 8:00 a.m., September 10, 1942. Betty, a long-time friend of Nancy's, was also long on experience, having logged 1,200 flight hours.

Nancy sent Betty out with an instructor for a flight test in the PT-19 trainer. When Betty returned to Nancy Love's office, she had passed her flight test. Off went Betty for the required Army physical, which she also passed. She signed up for the initial ninety-day appointment to the Women's Auxiliary Ferrying Squadron (WAFS). Nancy Love was WAFS #1. Betty Gillies was WAFS #2.

Cornelia Fort arrived later that same morning. After meeting with Nancy Love, she too was flight tested in the PT-19. Like Betty, she passed with flying colors. Ditto with the physical. Cornelia was the second woman Nancy hired to ferry aircraft, thus becoming WAFS #3. When she joined the WAFS, Cornelia's logbook showed her to have flown an impressive 924 hours.

Next to arrive were Helen Mary Clark, Aline "Pat" Rhonie, Catherine Slocum, Esther Nelson, Del Scharr, and Teresa James. On September 21, the WAFS number stood at nine. All were issued khaki flight coveralls in men's sizes, parachutes, goggles, and leather helmets (they would be flying open cockpit aircraft some of the time), a white silk U.S. Army Air Forces scarf, and a leather flight jacket.

Nancy Love leads her first eight recruits to the PT-19s they will be ferrying. From left: Teresa James, Cornelia Fort, Esther Nelson, Betty Gillies, Aline "Pat" Rhonie, Del Scharr is hidden behind Rhonie, then Helen Mary Clark, Nancy Love, and Catherine Slocum. *Courtesy Sarah Lawrence College Archives*

The WAFS home-away-from-home for the duration was BOQ 14 – Bachelor Officers' Quarters at New Castle Army Air Base.

The morning of September 22, the nine women were up at 6:45 and on duty at 8:00. The next day, September 23, the WAFS' thirty-day orientation began. Women continued to come, apply, pass their flight tests, and sign up to become civilian pilots in the history-making Women's Auxiliary Ferrying Squadron.

Cornelia and the other WAFS – all skilled, experienced pilots – were well aware of the fine line drawn between the traditional view of women and the revolutionary picture they presented flying airplanes. And now they were flying military aircraft – a job considered suitable only for men.

Many of the men in the Air Transport Command had great respect for these women pilots, but another group was openly and frankly antagonistic. As women everywhere know, the WAFS had to prove themselves daily.

Soon after joining the WAFS, Cornelia wrote:

> *Any girl who has flown at all grows used to the prejudice of most men pilots who will trot out any number of reasons why women can't possibly be good pilots. We grow so used to it in fact that I seldom think of it and almost never get on the defensive, as I did right after I soloed and wanted so desperately to be a good pilot.*
>
> *I was most fortunate to have good advice given me by the two men responsible both for my flying ability and my love of flying. The only way to show the disbelievers, the snickering hangar pilots, is to show them. And because the confidence in my flying of those two men, who were excellent pilots, came slowly and surely to be reflected in my flying, I gained early the strength not to care about the others.*

"When we all assembled in Wilmington, it was like we spoke different languages," said Gertrude Meserve, who arrived on September 30. "Florene with her Texas drawl, Nancy Batson and her even more leisurely Alabama drawl, Jamesy with her slangy Pittsburghese, me from Baahston."

Admission to the squadron required that they be high school graduates. As it turned out, finishing school and attendance at one of the exclusive Eastern women's colleges tied some of the earliest arrivals together. And, like Cornelia, several women had learned to fly because they came from well-off families and could afford the expense of flying lessons. Some even owned their own airplane.

Two exceptions were Teresa James and Del Scharr. At twenty-eight and thirty-four years old, respectively, they were from middle-class families and had been flying professionally as flight instructors and barnstormers (stunt flying in public events) for several years as a way to earn a living. As the younger women like Nancy Batson and Gertrude Meserve arrived, both twenty-two, the mix became more diverse.

A mixed group they may have been, but they began to bond.

Teresa in later years delighted in telling the story of a BOQ 14 bull session where some of the women bragged about their impressive alma maters. Nancy Love and Barbara Donahue both attended Vassar College, one of the famed Seven Sisters – elite women's colleges in the northeastern part of the United States. Cornelia, of course, had spent two years at the prestigious Sarah Lawrence College in Bronxville, New York. Then Betty and Cornelia – more than ten years apart in age – discovered they both attended The Ogontz School, the fashionable finishing school in Philadelphia that was also Amelia Earhart's prep school alma mater.

By then, Colonel Baker had announced that once the women had received their official uniforms, like the men on the base, they would be required to march in the Saturday morning review, even though they were civilians. Most of the women groaned over that announcement. Then Betty and Cornelia revealed with some degree of pride that they already knew how to march in formation. "No sweat," they might have said, recalling those days of relentless marching that, when pushed to admit it, both had totally despised.

"I was a drill sergeant at Ogontz," petite Betty – now thirty-four and the mother of two in elementary school – told the gathering. "We marched on the hockey field and carried heavy fake guns made of wood."

"We were the only girls' school I know of with military battalions – three of them," Cornelia chimed in. "And Betty, now I'm finding out you were one of those mean drill sergeants!"

"I should have been kicked out of that school for the things I did," Betty admitted, laughing at her memories of a misspent youth. "The seniors at Ogontz got to have parties in the woods, and we undergrads would slip out and heckle them. We climbed down the slate roof to where the garbage truck came in and slid down from there. One night we got caught. The headmistress threatened to stay in my room all night to keep me there 'unless you promise you won't go out again.' I said 'Miss Sutherland, I promise I won't go out.'"

Cornelia added her two cents to the revelation. "Well, I crawled out a window in biology class to avoid having to dissect a frog!"

Teresa cleared her throat. She'd had it with all this finishing school talk. "I always thought the education to be had at Thorne Hill was the absolute best money could buy."

That brought the conversation to a standstill.

Then, slowly, a chorus of courteous nods went around the circle. No one else seemed familiar with that particular school and, for several of them their social upbringing and impeccable manners showing, everyone was too polite to ask for clarification.

Quiet, shy Gertrude Meserve sat looking intently at Teresa, barely managing to hide her grin and smother her infectious giggle, but she didn't say a word. Only her raised eyebrows might have given her away. She had heard of Thorne Hill and knew Teresa was pulling their legs. But Gert didn't blow her cover.

The story came out years later when Teresa finally admitted, "Thorne Hill is a correctional school for boys in Pittsburgh. But I got tired of all the fancy talk about Wellesley, Vassar, and Smith. Then when Betty and Cornelia started exclaiming over this Ogontz School, I couldn't control myself." And she hooted with laughter at the memory.

"Only Jamesy with her raucous sense of humor could have pulled it off," said Gertrude.

And that was how it all began – women pilots from around the U.S.A. and all walks of life serving their country.

Chapter Eleven

Marching Does Not Come Easy!

NANCY BATSON FROM Birmingham, Alabama, came to Wilmington, Delaware, the minute she had sufficient hours – 503 – to qualify to join the WAFS. When the cab dropped her off at the guardhouse at the entrance to New Castle Army Air Base, the MP on duty took one look and rang a familiar number down on the flight line. He spoke into the telephone "Miz Love, I got another one."

When the Jeep delivered the attractive young woman to WAFS headquarters, Nancy Love invited her into her office. Within an hour, Nancy Batson was on her way out for her flight check in a PT-19, followed by the required physical. That afternoon, she qualified. Nancy's next stop was BOQ 14.

"I was sitting there on the cot in my room wondering what to do next when this tall brunette stuck her head in the door and introduced herself. 'I'm Cornelia Fort from Nashville,' she said. Her voice was deep but with a distinct Southern drawl. 'Would you like to come down to my room and have a cocktail, then go over to the Officers' Club for dinner?'

"Well, I was so delighted to hear another Southern accent, I said 'yes,' even though we didn't have cocktails in our home in Birmingham. Ladies in Birmingham didn't drink cocktails back then."

Cornelia's room was just down the hall from Nancy Batson's on the second floor of the BOQ. "I was fascinated by the array of liquor bottles lined up on the dresser. I felt quite sophisticated. When she asked me what I wanted, I said 'bourbon' like I had been drinking it for years."

Nancy Love, noting Nancy Batson's Southern birthright and wishing to make the young woman feel at ease, had asked her other Southern-born squadron member to look after her, introduce her to the other WAFS, and make her feel like one of them.

During the first month of the WAFS existence while undergoing their Army indoctrination before they began ferrying planes, the earliest arrivals had established a ritual. Nancy Love, Betty Gillies, Pat Rhonie, Helen Mary Clark, Cornelia Fort, and Catherine Slocum would gather at 4:30 p.m. in Nancy or Betty's room for cocktails.

Cocktail hour was a time-honored tradition in the homes of those wealthy, socially prominent women – with the exception of Cornelia, who was the daughter of a teetotaler. And, with the exception of Cornelia, all the others were married and older. But Cornelia had long ago thrown over the traces of her father's anti-alcohol crusade and cheerfully joined the other WAFS in the before-dinner cocktail hour.

That afternoon, more WAFS wandered into Cornelia's room, and she introduced them to Nancy Batson, the newest recruit. Then they all walked over to the Officers' Club together for dinner. Young, impressionable Nancy Batson appreciated Cornelia's friendliness and the fact that she reached out to a newcomer.

With the women's uniforms due to arrive soon, Colonel Baker told Nancy Love to get the women ready to march.

Nancy and her women pilots found themselves in for a challenge. Other than Betty and Cornelia's Ogontz School experience and Teresa's recent involvement in the Civil Air Patrol, marching was a new experience for the women. They couldn't get the hang of it. Betty, the confessed drill sergeant while in prep school, volunteered to teach them.

"Then there was Nancy Love's inability to develop a loud-mouthed 'hup, two, three, four' Marine drill sergeant style," WAFS Delphine Bohn later wrote in her memoir. "It caused her to develop occasional mental lapses when we were drilling."

Nancy Love freely admitted to her inadequacy. "We were obliged, among other routine indoctrination courses, to learn close-order drill. As Commander, I had to lead the formation and give the commands, which, because I was very self-conscious, was not one of my strong points.

"In fact, I so hated having to roar out orders that I occasionally drew a blank on what command to give next. This happened to me one dreary morning when we were drilling on an inactive runway. The squadron was marching smartly down the paved runway toward its end, where there was a sharp drop-off of about ten feet. Panic struck me as we approached the precipice and I found myself incapable of giving the command, 'To the rear – march!'

"So, off the girls went, still in close formation and roaring with laughter. Straight down the embankment they went and into the field, leaving me standing at the top, still speechless."

Finally, the WAFS, now in uniform and numbering twenty, joined the men on base for review.

Of that first morning review, Cornelia wrote:

For all the girls in the WAFS, I think the most concrete moment of happiness came at our first review. There was a backdrop of airplanes – hundreds of bombers parked neatly, awaiting foreign delivery. It was a quiet form of drama, but suddenly and for the first time we felt a part of something larger. Because of our uniforms, which we had earned, we were marching with the men, marching with all the freedom-loving people in the world.

And then while we were at attention a B-24 bomber took off, followed by four P-38 pursuit planes. We knew the bomber was headed across the ocean and that the fighters were to escort it part of the way. As they circled over us I could hardly see them for the tears in my eyes. It was striking symbolism and I think all of us felt it. As long as our planes flew overhead, the skies of America were free and that's what all of us everywhere were fighting for. And that we, in a very small way, are being allowed to help keep the sky free is the most beautiful thing I've ever known.

On October 19, 1942, at the end of the first thirty-day training period, eight WAFS graduated, making them eligible to ferry airplanes: Nancy Love, Betty Gillies, Cornelia Fort, Pat Rhonie, Helen Mary Clark, Del Scharr, Teresa James, and Catherine Slocum.

Cornelia was one of six WAFS assigned to make their first delivery. Six L4-B's (Piper Cubs known as *liaison aircraft*) needed to be moved from the Piper manufacturing plant in Lock Haven, Pennsylvania, to their delivery destination: Mitchel Field on Long Island, New York.

Nancy Love appointed her second in command, Betty Gillies, flight leader. Flying with Betty were Cornelia, Pat, Helen Mary, Del, and Teresa. It was their very first ferrying assignment.

Before they left – in preparation for flying as a group – Nancy Love gathered her WAFS and alerted them to ferrying's biggest "no-no." She warned them not to fly in formation like the male pilots. The women pilots were *not* headed for combat. They had *not* been taught formation flying and, in fact, now had strict orders from Nancy Love *not* to fly in formation.

"All the male cadets are taught to fly in close formation," Nancy told them. "They may be tempted to fly on your wing and horse around. That's against Civil Air Regulation, but they get by with it when they can. We haven't had the training. Stay at least five hundred feet away from each other."

For this trip, their first official outing, the WAFS wore their new uniform jackets and slacks under their flight coveralls. They packed their medium-heeled shoes, leather handbags with shoulder straps, and their uniform skirts in their Army-issue B-4 bags.

In 1942, the world was not used to seeing women in slacks. In fact, women in slacks were often refused entrance into restaurants – something the WAFS contended with early on. The only answer to a snobbish *maître d'* was for a WAFS attired in trousers to accept the snub, be turned away, and hope for a more liberal policy elsewhere. So when they could, they carried their skirts and dress shoes with them.

The WAFS were not out to prove they could wear pants. They only wanted to prove they could fly any airplane the military asked them to fly.

On October 22, the six ferry pilots, anxious to shake the down from their wings and fly for real, boarded a twin-engine transport, piloted by none other than Colonel Baker for the short flight to Lock Haven, Pennsylvania.

Both Cornelia and Teresa James wrote about the WAFS' first ferrying trip.

Cornelia wrote home:

Mother dearest,

It was tremendously exciting. We proceeded by an Army transport plane to Lock Haven, Pennsylvania, where the entire town was out to greet us. So somewhat self-consciously we climbed into six L4-Bs and took off across the Allegheny Mts. to Allentown where we "RONed – remained overnight".

Betty Gillies was Flight Leader and consequently brought up the rear to watch over the flight. I was sub-flight leader and was in front which is a somewhat awe-inspiring job. All of us felt practically historic – the first female ferry pilots to have active duty.

Our hotel was the height of luxury. Bathtubs instead of showers. Great soft beds instead of Army cots. And a telephone to wake us instead of pounding on doors.

The next morning we left precisely at 8 and arrived at our destination, Mitchel Field, Long Island, where we heaved a thankful sigh that our first mission was completed without incident.

Truth be told, the WAFS' first mission was not without incident.

In her daily journal, Teresa James wrote this about their landing at Mitchel Field: "As per Betty's orders, we were up at sunrise the next morning bound for Mitchel Field. Six little Cubs came in and made six perfect landings. We had made the trip in sixty-five minutes.

"Betty Gillies signed over the planes to a thunder-faced officer, who told her – in no uncertain terms – that he needed them two months ago, not now.

"That's not my problem," Betty said, sweetly. "I'm merely following orders. You may speak to my commanding officer, Colonel Robert Baker at New Castle Army Air Base, or call Colonel Tunner himself at Ferrying Division headquarters." She gave the man a big smile.

Considering the man's rudeness, and knowing Betty, all the women knew her smile was delivered around clenched teeth.

At that moment the phone rang. The man turned to answer it.

"The night before, when Betty had talked to her husband on the phone, he had warned her that bombing practice was planned the following day in the area where they would be flying. All flying was ordered grounded during the bombing. Betty immediately wired Mitchel Field operations to let them know the WAFS were flying in with deliveries that morning and to call off the guns until they could get the planes safely on the ground," Teresa wrote.

"The call turned out to be the telegram Betty had sent asking them to call off the bombing until the Cubs were safely in. *The call came several hours late!*

"Betty paled when she heard the news. But the Cubs were safely in, no thanks to either Western Union or Operations at Mitchel Field."

With her airplanes safely delivered, Betty won over the other men in Operations – ignoring the one who told her he didn't want the planes anymore. She enlisted the help of another man who readily succumbed to her polite smile and pleasant voice. She asked him to call for ground transportation for six WAFS to get them to the Aviation Country Club nearby.

"Betty and Pat Rhonie were members and, therefore, we all would be welcome," Teresa wrote.

Cornelia's letter to her mother continues:

> *We went with Betty Gillies to the famous Aviation Country Club (airport, swimming pool, tennis court, skeet shooting, and the other usual country club facilities) where we changed into our uniform skirts and had pre-lunch sherry to celebrate.*
>
> *Being very hungry for good music I streaked into NY to Carnegie Hall to hear Maestro Bruno Walter conduct, then met Bill's mother Mrs. McCain at "21" for a drink.*

Teresa's account is in full agreement:

"After that, we all split up for the next few hours. Scharr and I went to Radio City Music Hall. Gillies went home. Rhonie dashed off somewhere. Clark dashed off for Jersey to see her husband and two children. Fort called some friends. She was like a sailor – friends in every port."

Cornelia concludes with:

All of us took the 6:30 train home. It's simply wonderful to be able to whip out our little book of travel tickets and know we will get space by priority if necessary. Actually it is fair because having flown all day we need sleep and rest on the way home for the next trip. Our uniforms, which are as yet devoid of insignia, created a great stir. People guessed everything from Air Raid Wardens to WAACs [Women's Army Auxiliary Corps] to Junior (Girl Scout) Commandos.

Chapter Twelve

Now the Real Ferrying Begins

THE DAY AFTER CORNELIA and the other WAFS returned from their first ferrying trip, the brass of the Ferrying Division/Air Transport Command descended on New Castle Army Air Base to congratulate the returning heroines of the Mitchel Field delivery. Cornelia wrote a letter to her mother that evening:

> *Colonel Tunner, Commanding officer for the whole division, flew up from Washington to review us today. With all twenty of us in uniform, we presented quite a spectacle. Now we are on call for the next trip.*

And she added that General Harold George, Head of the Air Transport Command – Tunner's boss – paid the WAFS a visit as well. Cornelia was invited to sit at his table for lunch.

Most complimentary of their successful first full month on the job as well as their first delivery, the general confided in Cornelia, "Yes, the WAFS definitely will fly more than Piper Cubs and small trainers." True, it would take time, he told her, but "bigger stuff" (more challenging aircraft) was coming.

On November 11, 1942, Cornelia, Teresa James, and Betty Gillies were joined by four newly qualified WAFS – Barbara Poole, Helen Richards, Barbara Towne, and Barbara "BJ" Erickson to take seven Cubs south. This trip would be far longer than the flight to Mitchel Field. For the WAFS, the real ferrying had begun!

Unfortunately, when landing in Charlottesville, Virginia, to refuel they ran into a problem. The field had been under water for three weeks and was still a sea of mud. The WAFS were not warned of this.

Cornelia was leading the flight. When she landed, her aircraft nosed over in the muck, damaging the propeller. The others, noting her predicament from the air, took extra precaution not to do the same. It wasn't easy, but the rest got down safely.

Cornelia's bent propeller was hardly her fault, but she was grounded until it could be repaired. The other six, after refueling, went on without her. They had planes to deliver. Cornelia waved them off and got back to the business of getting her bent prop fixed. She RONed that night in Charlottesville.

When she left the following day, Cornelia pointed her Cub toward Atlanta, Georgia. Her intent was to RON (remain overnight) with her brother Dudley and his family who lived in Atlanta. The night of November 13, she did just that. To this day, Dudley, Jr. remembers his Aunt Cornelia's first visit "to him" while on her ferrying trips.

The following day, she delivered her Cub to Tuskegee, Alabama, home of the Tuskegee Airmen – a squadron of young, Black pilots in training there. They were headed abroad to fly fighter aircraft in Europe in the war against Nazi Germany. Some of them would be taking their initial training in the Cub that Cornelia delivered.

No sooner had she returned to base in Wilmington, she was assigned another trip out of Lock Haven. Cornelia, Betty, Barbara Towne, BJ, and Teresa headed for the Piper factory to pick up more Cubs and deliver them south.

RONing with the Marine Corps that night in Quantico, Virginia, the WAFS were invited out to dinner and then to the

Officers' Club. Teresa relates that the evening was most festive ¬– cocktails before dinner, wine with dinner, followed by some celebratory champagne. The major who ordered the champagne was in a particularly jovial mood.

The women had been given blocked-off quarters on one floor of the BOQ, and the men who belonged on that corridor were asked to make other arrangements. Of course, the inevitable happened. There was a mix-up of beds!

There was no hanky-panky. No one was breaking protocol or any other rules of conduct, but when Teresa made her way to the bed where she had carefully laid out her pajamas before leaving for dinner, she found the major. Yes, it was the same major who had supplied the champagne. He was clad only in his shorts and was snoring away.

Teresa sought out the corporal who had led the five women to these quarters in the first place. "Would you please evict the major from my cot?!"

"He's a major. I'm only a corporal," the very upset young man insisted. He backed swiftly out of the room, refusing to have any part in this drama.

An equally upset Teresa finally managed to snake her pajamas out from under the major – the movement did not disturb him in the least – and went with the corporal to find another room.

The long-suffering corporal deposited Teresa in Cornelia's room, because it was empty. Cornelia, who like the major, had drunk a little bit too much champagne, was in the shower trying to clear her head. When she got back to the room she found Teresa in her bed.

Now what?

Cornelia simply returned to the shower room. There, she had noticed a single bathtub in the far corner. She stretched her five-foot ten-inch frame out in that tub. She was a veteran of Eastern girls' school parties. Those young ladies frequently stayed overnight in New York hotels after festivities in the Big Apple. They quickly learned that a bathtub could be a useful, if not the most comfortable, substitute for a bed, particularly if one had had just a bit too much to drink.

When the major awoke the following morning, he acted quite nonchalant, as if no mistake had been made. His quarters, Teresa learned, were actually one floor below, which accounted for the mix-up.

The weather on the morning of November 19 kept them grounded until noon. They took off for Winston-Salem, North Carolina, where they RONed. The next day, the weather was so bad, the best they could do was 150 miles. They RONed in Spartanburg, South Carolina.

Finally, the night of November 21, Cornelia landed again in Atlanta where she spent the night with Dudley and his family. She presented Dudley, Jr. and his siblings with a cap pistol featuring the popular 1940s comic-strip character Dick Tracy.

Author's note: Dudley, Jr., told this author on August 5, 2022, that his father, Dudley senior (Cornelia's brother), immediately confiscated the cap pistol and put it up on the mantel, out of reach. He gave strict orders not to shoot it. But Dudley, Jr. and his siblings managed to get the prized cap pistol off the mantel and, with great delight, took it outside and had a ball shooting up the neighborhood with caps that went "BANG" but hurt no one.

Dudley, Jr. also recalled that Aunt Cornelia promised on her next visit to bring her parachute for them to see.

Cornelia delivered her Piper Cub to Biloxi, Mississippi, then it was back to New Castle Army Air Base and BOQ 14.

By the end of November 1942, the WAFS had ferried forty Piper L-4B Cubs and ten Fairchild PT-19s to flight training facilities throughout the eastern and southern portions of the nation. In

At Nashville's Berry Field, Cornelia Fort signs over her L-4B liaison (J-3 Cub) for safekeeping, so she can RON that night with her family in Nashville. *Courtesy WASP Archives, Texas Woman's University*

December, they would ferry twenty-four more Cubs and four more PT-19s. That women could handle these assignments was obvious.

Finally, one of Cornelia's December Cub-delivery flights took her to Nashville. Much to her delight, she got to spend the night of December 20 at Fortland. The family gathered to welcome this near stranger to their midst – an early Christmas present.

The next morning, Cornelia picked up her Cub, took off, and delivered it to its final destination, Dyersburg, Tennessee, seventy-nine miles northeast of Memphis. It had been good to have at least a short visit with her family. Back to the base in Wilmington.

+++

That fall, while Nancy Love and her WAFS were getting acquainted with ferrying small army aircraft, another well-known woman pilot, Jacqueline Cochran, had been working with Army Air Forces Commanding General Henry "Hap" Arnold to establish a flight training school for women pilots. The school was now in operation at the municipal airport in Houston, Texas, where more female pilots ages twenty-one to thirty-five were being trained to fly "the Army way."

Once the women completed the curriculum and earned their wings, they would join the WAFS and begin ferrying U.S. military aircraft around the United States and into Canada. How soon this would happen was uncertain. Much depended on how quickly the first class of women completed their training course.

When the WAFS squadron at New Castle Army Air Base reached its recommended strength of twenty-five – and knowing that eventually the women graduating from the flight training school in Texas would be swelling their ranks – the Ferrying Division made plans to form more WAFS ferrying units. During December 1942, Nancy Love visited the other six ferrying bases already housing male ferrying squadrons. Would they accept a female squadron? Three of the bases said "yes."

WAFS squadrons would be established with the 5th Ferrying Group at Love Field in Dallas, Texas; the 3rd Ferrying Group at Wayne County Airport in Romulus, Michigan, near Detroit; and the 6th Ferrying Group at the Long Beach, California, airport.

No one knew when the flight school in Texas would turn out its first graduates, but when it did, those women were destined to fly with the WAFS. This meant the number of women ferry pilots would grow, and the Ferrying Division had to get ready for them.

Nancy Love went to work. By the end of December, she had organized what would now be her four WAFS squadrons. From her current pool of twenty-five highly experienced pilots, she planned to send five women to each of the three bases to establish the new squadrons. The other ten WAFS would remain at Wilmington where the ferrying schedule already was established and functioning well.

When the women pilots being trained in Texas graduated, they would be divided among the four WAFS squadrons.

Nancy was well aware of the Ferrying Division's plans for the coming year. Colonel Tunner had kept her informed. She knew her growing number of women ferry pilots would be asked to fly bigger and more complex aircraft. To prepare for this, she had the Colonel's blessing to fly and check out on any aircraft she felt she was capable of flying. This would show the Army Air Force's higher command that a woman could, in fact, handle bigger aircraft. Nancy had no qualms about checking out in every aircraft on the list.

At the end of December 1942, Nancy turned the Wilmington squadron over to her second-in-command and close friend, Betty Gillies. Nancy headed to Dallas, Texas, to establish the first of her new women's squadrons.

In Houston, by the end of December 1942, eighty women pilots were learning to fly "the Army way." Cornelia's friend from Honolulu, Betty Guild (married name Tackaberry) was in the very first class, numbering twenty-nine.

✈ ✈ ✈

Cornelia and her sister WAFS were itching to get their hands on the bigger airplanes General George had promised – basic trainers (BT), advanced trainers (AT), and twin-engine aircraft. In addition, they had seen an occasional fighter plane, the P-47, on the flight line at Wilmington and watched the men take off in a roar, flying the big plane into the wild blue yonder. They had heard tales of the big "Jug's" awesome might when the men returned the 2,000-horsepower monster to earth. The women lusted to get their hands on the controls of those brutes of the air.

Having had the joy of spending all that incredibly fun time in the Waco doing aerobatics, Cornelia, too, was ready for bigger, heavier, faster airplanes.

Long Beach, California, is where Cornelia hoped to be sent. The women stationed there would ferry the Vultee BT-13 – the Army's basic trainer. And many more aircraft factories were close by including North American, which built the awesome P-51 fighters. Cornelia and all the other WAFS wanted to fly a P-51 in the worst way.

Before Nancy Love left for Dallas, she told Cornelia "yes," she was being assigned to Long Beach.

Chapter Thirteen

Fortland Burns to the Ground

DEL SCHARR AND CORNELIA had become friends. Fate, so to speak, had thrown them together. Both standing five feet ten inches, they were the two tallest WAFS. When the women began marching, the two became, in Del's words, "marching buddies." They brought up the rear – or led when Nancy Love, now more at home with the process, gave the command "to the rear march."

On the night of December 27, 1942, Del was in her room in BOQ 14 writing a letter to her husband when, suddenly, she sensed someone's presence. She looked up and saw Cornelia standing in the open doorway, looking like a ghost.

Del wrote in her memoir, *Sisters in the Sky*, "Cornelia was holding onto the door jamb. Then she spoke. 'I've had a telephone call from home – Fortland just burned to the ground.'"

Del was stunned by the news. "Oh, Cornelia! was all I could say as tears came to my eyes."

"No one was injured," she told Del. "No one was in residence at the time, but everything is gone." Cornelia choked back a sob and went on. "All my diaries are gone. I just sent them home last week – for safekeeping."

Suspecting that she might be transferred to one of the new squadrons, Cornelia had decided not to take her precious diaries

Cornelia watches as Lieutenant Starbuck helps WAFS Barbara Poole get her open cockpit PT-19 started. *Courtesy the WASP Archives, Texas Woman's University*

with her. But now fire had destroyed them along with everything else in the house.

"That's when I learned that, from the day she began to fly, Cornelia had fashioned a chronicle of her life in aviation," Del wrote. "Of the WAFS, she was certainly the one most qualified to write about us. She was an avid reader, she expressed herself well, and she had the patience to sit alone and write her thoughts while the rest of us either relaxed or ran about socially. No wonder

Cornelia had not joined us at our end of the barracks – she had her work to do, a serious task for one so young in years."

Del also recalled how in control Cornelia managed to stay when talking about the fire.

"She showed some emotion to me, but she did not break down about her loss in front of the others. She had a certain nobility; she possessed quality and breeding. Now, tragedy had threatened her life twice. First she escaped death at Pearl Harbor. Now she had escaped the fire at Fortland. But the carefully recorded hours and years of her career were only cinders.

"Pilots are superstitious," Del wrote. "They believe that bad luck comes in threes. If there have been two accidents from one airport, for instance, everyone breathes easier once the third has happened."

+ + +

Cornelia's first PT-19 delivery was scheduled to take off December 31, 1942. That morning, she and several other WAFS were flown to the Fairchild Aviation factory in Hagerstown, Maryland, to pick up their aircraft.

Still with a heavy heart over the news of Fortland, Cornelia climbed into the open cockpit (no canopy and it was December!) and settled herself in.

She was wearing bulky, Army-issue winter flying gear – as dressed for the weather as it was possible to be. The first layer consisted of long, scratchy, woolen underwear and layers of socks. Over the long johns she pulled on high-waisted, fleece-lined leather pants. These zipped from the shinbone of one leg up to the sternum and were held in place by suspenders. She topped that with a fleece-lined leather jacket.

Because of the open cockpit, the WAFS were issued leather flying caps with chin straps, goggles, fleece-lined leather gloves, and wool-lined boots. "I thought, surely, all this would be enough to keep the cold out, but it wasn't," Cornelia wrote to her mother that evening. "To that, I added my parachute, with straps over the shoulders and around the thighs."

The final addition was a chamois mask held in place by wide, black, elastic bands. The mask provided some semblance of protection against frostbite, because of the frigid air aloft. From her experience flying the PT-19 during orientation earlier that fall, Cornelia already knew that when flying an open cockpit trainer, a runny nose was a constant companion.

The WAFS quickly learned that flying in an open cockpit in a small, vulnerable aircraft in the depth of winter was an unimaginable challenge. Cornelia could barely feel her fingers and toes throughout the flight.

Their first destination was Lynchburg, Virginia, where they RONed. When they took off the morning of January 1, 1943, Cornelia left the group and headed once again for Atlanta. She planned to RON there and spend the rest of New Year's day with her brother Dudley and his family.

Dudley, Jr. was overjoyed to see his Aunt Cornelia again, but he was disappointed that she forgot to bring her parachute along to show him. She had promised. "Next trip," she said.

Eighty years later, Dudley still remembers that promise.

The next day Cornelia flew on to Birmingham, Alabama, and then Jackson, Mississippi; Shreveport, Louisiana; Dallas, Texas; and finally Vernon, Texas – her delivery destination for a very long trip.

On January 6, when Cornelia returned from her first open cockpit ferrying trip – mostly in the freezing cold – she found a disturbing letter waiting for her.

After Christmas, she had written to her mother with news of Bill – her admirer from her time in Honolulu. Bill had presented her with a perfectly lovely gold bracelet. She added that Bill was pressuring her to marry him.

Mrs. Fort, upset by the expensive gift and the marriage proposal, wrote back to Cornelia, scolding her for keeping the bracelet. She demanded that her daughter return it.

Cornelia was not feeling well following her six-day trip in the frigid winter weather.

Like all the WAFS, Cornelia was under considerable pressure to perform in her job. She was a professional. The planes they ferried were badly needed for the war effort. That's why they were flying them. Their schedule was extremely demanding and, yes, the East Coast's foul weather made flying anywhere a perilous proposition.

Now she had family problems as well.

January 7, 1943, was Betty Gillies's thirty-fifth birthday. That evening, Cornelia joined her squadron leader and friend to celebrate by having dinner with her at the Hotel du Pont in Wilmington. Betty could see Cornelia was distressed. Was she ill, or was it something else?

The next day, Betty called the base doctor to take a look at her.

After Cornelia had RONed with her brother Dudley and his family the evening of January 1, 1943, Dudley wrote home to their mother that his sister was under a great deal of strain, and he thought she should resign from the WAFS.

That night she spent in Atlanta, he flatly told her, "You've done enough for your country."

The miserable conditions of flying in an open cockpit and now the additional stress from that unsolicited advice from her brother, along with this unexpected reaction from her mother, all had to have played a huge part in her deteriorating condition. The doctor put Cornelia on sick leave. Betty ordered her to go home to recuperate. Cornelia didn't want to leave the base, but Betty was adamant.

Cornelia went home to Nashville. The family wondered if she might have had some sort of breakdown.

After she regained some of her strength, Cornelia and her mother took a short vacation to Florida where it was mild and sunny. Apparently both benefited from the warmth and the time they spent together.

When she arrived back in Wilmington at the end of January, Cornelia wrote her mother:

> *Not a word from Bill. He must really have the sulks. I returned the bracelet and felt like a damned fool. I'm sure he doesn't want it back, but I guess it's better.*

Cornelia wanted to ferry more PTs, but Betty was cautious. She wanted her to ease back into the routine given her lengthy recuperation. Cornelia spent the first week back on the Link Trainer.

On February 5, 1943, her twenty-fourth birthday, she wrote the following to her mother, admitted to her tiredness and remembering to thank her for her birthday present:

> *I'm a birthday girl and never felt less so. I feel about 104 instead of 24. . . . The slip is breathtaking. I'll feel as flossy as Mae West when I put it on under my uniform.*

On February 8, Cornelia was back in the rotation. Fortunately, her first assignment was in a PT-26. This aircraft was identical to the PT-19 except that it had a canopy, therefore an enclosed cockpit. She wasn't directly exposed to the nasty winter weather that was plaguing the entire northeastern United States.

Back to Hagerstown. This trip, Cornelia and five other WAFS took their PT-26s north. After refueling in Niagara Falls, New York, they delivered their aircraft to Malton, Ontario, Canada. They RONed there, then home to New Castle Army Air Base on February 10.

Finally, the day Cornelia had been waiting for!

The time had come for the WAFS assigned to Long Beach to head west. BJ Erickson, appointed squadron commander, was already out there setting up so her sister WAFS could join her. Also assigned to Long Beach were Evelyn Sharp, Barbara Towne, and Bernice Batten.

Cornelia took an overnight trip to Nashville before flying west. She actually went on a fox hunt in the snow the afternoon she arrived. Then she spent a quiet evening with her mother. The next day she flew to California.

In Long Beach at last, on February 15, 1943, Cornelia and the other four WAFS were introduced to the BT-13, the U.S. Army Air Forces basic trainer. It had a big 450-horsepower engine, low-wing like the PT-19 but, thankfully, it had a closed canopy. And, it had a radio! This was a very big step up – communication with the ground while in flight!

On February 18, Cornelia and the others took off on their first BT-13 trip from Downey, California, home of the Vultee factory where the BT-13s were built. Destination Dallas, Texas. They were back in Long Beach on February 22, just in time for a memorable event that would "live in infamy" for the five Long Beach WAFS.

On February 23, 1943, they were introduced to the very jealous wives of the men they were serving alongside.

Cornelia wrote this in her diary:

It was the most desperate ordeal I ever saw. Talk about being stared at and appraised and in a decidedly unfriendly fashion. Whew! They are in a frenzy of jealousy we will copilot with their husbands. Of all the damned, stupid, female rot!

Colonel Spake sent his Deputy, Major Dunlap, to make a speech – which had a dual purpose. Theoretically it was a speech of welcome for us. Actually it was an announcement to the wives that they need not worry, that no "mixed" operations orders would be issued, i.e., no man and girl as pilot and copilot.

Those rude women applauded right in front of us! Can you believe it?! I was so livid at the exhibition, whose equal I've never seen, that I got up and walked out – whereupon the other girls followed me. I hope those women had the grace to be ashamed of their rudeness, if not their feelings.

The following day the WAFS were off in their BT-13s. This time their delivery point was San Antonio, Texas.

On February 27, Cornelia wrote:

Back in Long Beach! Nancy [Love] came out to be guinea pig for us Long Beach WAFS. She checked out in a P-51 [Mustang] and a C-47 [wartime designation for the DC-3 airliner] all in one day. What a great day for the females!

Yes! That day, Nancy Love made history.

Colonel Tunner's approval to fly anything she felt she was capable of flying had paid off. She was the first woman pilot to check out in and fly the P-51 Mustang – the pursuit aircraft that would soon become the United States' premier fighter of World War II.

More than 130 of Nancy's women ferry pilots would follow her and qualify to ferry not only the P-51 but all the other single-engine, pursuit fighters in the U.S. World War II arsenal.

All the pursuits just had a single seat in the cockpit! Your first flight in this powerful fighter is a solo!

Ten days later, Betty Gillies – Nancy's second-in-command who also had Colonel Tunner's nod of approval to fly anything she wanted to fly – was the first woman to check out in and fly the P-47 Thunderbolt, the largest pursuit aircraft built by the U.S. The WAFS were on their way.

The WAFS were going to fly the "big stuff."

Chapter Fourteen

Where's Your Short Snorter?

THE ORIGINAL MEANING OF "short snorter" was "a little less than a full drink at a bar." That tradition, begun in the 1920s by Alaskan bush pilots, spread as military and commercial aviation developed between World Wars I and II.

Cornelia's short snorter *Courtesy Cornelia Fort Papers, Special Collections Division, Nashville Public Library; Photo by Judith Miller*

In WWII – thanks to the creation and mission of the Air Transport Command – "short snorter" took on new meaning. The men of the ATC flew to every corner of the world, delivering desperately needed airplanes and supplies. They all carried "short snorters" – a roll of bills (paper currency) taped together end-to-end. The longer your short snorter, the more countries you had visited. A badge of honor! And they signed each other's short snorters.

If a man signed your short snorter and then could not produce his own short snorter upon request, he owed you a dollar – or a drink.

The signatures the men collected on paper currency from around the globe came to resemble an autograph book. Wherever they gathered, the men produced their short snorters with pride.

Stationed with the 6th Ferrying Group in Long Beach, Cornelia and the other four WAFS were in the midst of a major aviation center of the worldwide ATC action. When the WAFS began to meet and mix with their fellow male ferry pilots, they learned about short snorters.

Those young male ferry pilots literally were off to see the world or just back from seeing it. The women, envious, loved to talk to the guys and listen to them talk about where they had been. Cornelia and the other WAFS, eager to be in on the fun, began to assemble their own short snorters.

But the women pilots were relegated to strictly stateside duty or an occasional ferrying trip to Canada. To build their own short snorters, they collected coveted foreign currency from the men whenever they could.

In addition to U.S. dollar bills, Cornelia's short snorter included currency from Cuba, Mexico, and other foreign countries. The currency notes are autographed by men with whom she shared a cocktail, a cup of coffee, dinner, a conversation, a dance. It was a badge of honor for both the male and the female ferry pilots, and they all carried their short snorters with pride.

And it wasn't just ferry pilots and aircrews who carried short snorters, it was service-wide. First Lady Eleanor Roosevelt was known to carry her own short snorter – and it remained dear to her long after the war was over. Cornelia and the WAFS were in good company.

+++

As Teresa James once observed, Cornelia was like a sailor, she had friends everywhere!

She also liked having a good time. Here are highlights from Cornelia's Long Beach diary, February and March 1943:

> *February 27, Dinner with Nancy and the great Andy Cannon (just back from a B-24 trip to Africa), etc. at the Club.* (Colonel Cannon, an old friend and confidant of Nancy and Bob Love, would soon take command of the base in Long Beach.)
>
> *March 1, Another Palm Springs RON. Dinner with Sanchez after a swim and a ramble around listening to some fancy piano playing.*
>
> *March 3, Into Dallas with the afternoon free. Finally saw Casablanca [a 1942 movie]. Airlines home. And a very adventurous airline ride it was. A routine 7 hour run took 27 hours. 21 tired pilots delivered back to Long Beach. But not too tired for a dinner out on the town.*
>
> *March 4, Dinner at Leilani with Nancy, Sam Dunlap and Andy Cannon, etc. The atmosphere and the Hawaiian music made me suddenly and acutely homesick for the islands. Such a lost beautiful world.*
>
> *March 5, Lunch in L.A with Clarence Belinn who is off for Honolulu. I felt like a lady (instead of a WAFS) again having cocktails at the most-nice Town House before lunch of green salad and French pastry.*
>
> *March 6, To Hollywood "Satiddy-Nightin" with Hugh Martin. Cocktails at the Ambassador and a very lush dinner – Guinea hen in wine with black cherries.*

March 7, Green salad and French pastry at the Officers' Club.

March 8, No trip – all day at the base. A drink with Colonel Andy Cannon and Major Sam Dunlap, two fireball officers who really run the Post.

Cornelia was having the time of her life – and then it got even better.

March 9, Quite an eventful day. Bought a dream car, grey Chevy convertible which will be wonderful fun here in California.

In her diary the next day, Cornelia noted that Nancy Love and BJ Erickson had returned from their first C-47 trip. This was an important feat on the part of these two top-rated WAFS pilots. The C-47 – a twin-engine passenger plane known before the war as the DC-3 – had been converted to wartime use as a cargo and troop transport plane.

This was a big step up for the WAFS, as it appeared that they soon would be flying twin-engine aircraft. Things definitely were looking up. The women were proving they were capable of flying far more than small training aircraft. They were well on their way to flying bigger, heavier, faster warplanes.

Continuing in her diary, Cornelia wrote:

March 10, Great news! Nancy Love is being transferred to Long Beach.

March 11, I drove my little buggy – top down – to L.A. Had dinner at the Cock 'n' Bull, all sorts of British things – Welsh rarebit, beef and kidney pie, turkey curry, artichoke and trifle. Marvelous place and better food.

March 12, Friday: Sat on the green California grass in the bright California sun. Drove top down to Pasadena with Peter. Lay on the floor in front of the fire after dinner, toasting marshmallows – Ah joy!

In a letter to her brother Garth, she wrote:

I love everything about the post [Long Beach], the people, the planes, and my gray convertible.

Back to work on March 16, Cornelia took a BT-13 on a short hop from Downey to Lemoore, California. On March 17 and 19 she logged time in the Link Trainer on the base.

Cornelia, who once upon a time lived in a self-fashioned shell, was feeling her oats and allowing herself to escape that shell. She was experiencing a new-found freedom.

The Long Beach WAFS squadron: Seated on the wing of a BT-13 are Cornelia Fort, Evelyn Sharp, and squadron commander BJ Erickson. Standing (left) Barbara Towne, (right) Bernice Batten. *Courtesy Sarah Lawrence College Archives*

Chapter Fifteen

Cornelia, Please Don't Do It!

ON THE MORNING OF MARCH 20, 1943, several BT-13s were parked on the tarmac at the Vultee factory, ready for delivery. The five Long Beach WAFS watched as male ferry pilots took off in six of them on a BT delivery to Dallas.

Plans that morning called for a WAFS photo session. The picture taken of the five women would appear with an article in *Air Age* magazine in August.

Cornelia, Evelyn Sharp, and BJ Erickson sat lined up on the right wing of one of the planes. Barbara Towne and Bernice Batten stood below, flanking the three on the wing.

Cornelia's assignment also was to deliver a 450-horsepower BT-13 Vultee Valiant to Love Field in Dallas. The BT definitely was a step up for the WAFS, and this was Cornelia's fifth trip in the BT. She wrote to a friend: "I know the route to Dallas so well now I've cut a groove in the sky."

When the picture taking was done, Cornelia climbed into the cockpit, waved to the other WAFS, and took off. She got as far as Tucson, Arizona, where the fading daylight made it necessary for her to RON. The following morning – Sunday, March 21 – she headed for Dallas Love Field.

She landed in Midland, Texas, at 12:45 p.m. to refuel and grab a bite of lunch. There, she ran into the male BT-13 ferry pilots also out of Long Beach and headed for Dallas. She joined the group. The men were discussing formation flying.

The Army Air Forces trained its young male pilots headed for combat to fly in a tactical formation. Close, but still loosely spaced, they were able to see each other's planes and spot each other's blind spots. This made it difficult for an enemy plane to target and isolate any one of their aircraft. Flying in this formation offered these young, relatively inexperienced pilots a mutual defense and a concentration of firepower.

Did Nancy Love's words from the previous October – "Stay at least five hundred feet away from each other" echo in Cornelia's head?

Cornelia was a skilled pilot – she had more than 1,000 hours in the air! She had far more experience than any of these young men she was talking with. She also thrived on challenge and appeared to have an unquenchable thirst for excitement – and for danger. Taking chances did not deter her from doing what she wanted to do.

What happened next is unclear.

Did the guys talk Cornelia into joining them and flying close formation? Did she, wishing to be one of the guys, opt in? She very well may have agreed to join in the fun. Or did she say, "thanks but no thanks"?

Only the pilots in the air that day knew what actually happened.

+++

When researching Cornelia's story in the 1990s, Rob Simbeck, author of *Daughter of the Air*, located and interviewed one of the male pilots who was part of that March 1943 ferrying assignment. With Rob's permission, I am using information from that interview here as well as other facts Rob uncovered.

The pilot Rob interviewed recalled that Cornelia was a little hesitant, but said she would like to try formation flying. Another pilot suggested she could simply continue to fly straight and level. The men would fly on her wing and only they would change positions in flight.

One of the men refused to take part in any of this. Did he recognize the danger – the possibility for disaster? He left the group immediately and took off for Dallas.

After refueling their aircraft, the remaining pilots – six including Cornelia – took off for Dallas.

The pilot continued with his recollection: "We were headed eastward flying formation. The men changed position in flight, moving from her [Cornelia's] right wing to her left wing. We weren't any too close – just the way we would have been in training. We were young and full of vinegar, and none of us ever considered the possible consequences."

His job was to send periodic radio reports back to base at Long Beach, giving their position as they headed for Dallas. He pulled some distance away and positioned himself to the side of the other aircraft in order to radio in his report. While there, he noticed one of the male pilots flying too close to Cornelia's aircraft.

He told Rob, "Moments later, Cornelia's plane suddenly broke off to the right and began to roll."

Her plane did not come out of that roll, nor did she bail out of the plane. Cornelia's BT-13 crashed into the rough, tangled Texas terrain.

The remaining planes circled the crash site. Already, local residents were headed toward the crash site. Nothing moved.

Seeing help was on the way, the men flew on to Dallas to complete their ferrying mission.

It took time for an investigating officer to reach the site. When he arrived, he took charge of the accident scene. It was some time before he was able to locate and talk with the flight leader. When he did, that pilot gave him this description of the accident: "Immediately after the collision, Cornelia's plane rolled over several times, then went into an inverted dive rotating slowly to the left until it slammed vertically into the ground."

Cornelia's plane did not burn. When the aircraft hit the ground, it buried itself several feet into the red Texas soil. Both wing tanks had just been refilled. The investigating officer concluded that, because the engine was so quickly buried, the fuel failed to ignite. That's why there was no fire.

His conclusion: One of the male pilots had performed a roll above Cornelia's aircraft. As he completed the maneuver, the landing gear of his BT-13 struck the left wing of Cornelia's aircraft, peeling six feet off the front section of the wing. The investigating officer subsequently reported that when the initial impact occurred, apparently it either knocked Cornelia unconscious or killed her instantly. Either way, she died in the resulting crash.

The investigation's conclusion would make no difference in the final outcome. Cornelia Clark Fort – the third woman pilot to sign on with the Women's Auxiliary Ferrying Squadron to help defend the United States after the Japanese attack at Pearl Harbor – was dead.

✈ ✈ ✈

Word of Cornelia's death spread rapidly through the WAFS squadrons and, because of her celebrity from Pearl Harbor, was big news across America.

The storm clouds that erupted from what happened in that remote site in the state of Texas on March 21, 1943, could have shut the WAFS down. Many military men in command positions would have gladly stopped the women from flying right then and there.

Fortunately, more reasonable heads – the men responsible for the WAFS – prevailed. ATC commander General Harold George, his second-in-command General C.R. Smith, and WAFS commanding officer Colonel William H. Tunner, knew the scarcity of men available to perform the ferrying jobs that had to be done. And they knew those experienced women pilots had the ability to do this kind of flying. The women pilots were needed. There was a war on.

WAFS leader Nancy Love, along with BJ Erickson – Cornelia's commanding officer at Long Beach – and Major Sam Dunlap, Long Beach air base second-in-command, flew a twin-engine C-47 to Nashville to attend Cornelia's funeral.

BJ wrote to her parents describing the trip and meeting the Fort family.

> *Wednesday (March 24th) Major Dunlap, Nancy and I flew to Nashville, arriving there at 5:30 a.m. Thursday morning. It was bad weather most of the way and Major D. did most of the flying. Nancy and I alternated flying copilot and trying to sleep on the floor in the navigator's place.*
>
> *When we arrived, it took quite a while to finally get a hotel room, as nearly everything was full, but finally did. We cleaned up, ate breakfast and by that time it was 8:30 – so we called Mrs. Fort for we knew she was waiting to hear we all had arrived OK.*
>
> *We arrived at the funeral home about 10 and met Mrs. Fort and all the family. Naturally they wanted to know everything and we couldn't tell them anything because we didn't know anything.*

The Army had released no information and Nancy, BJ, and Major Dunlap were as much in the dark as the family regarding details of the accident. Mrs. Fort then asked the three of them – all wearing their official dress uniforms – to lead the mourners up the aisle at Nashville's Christ Episcopal Church.

Because of the prominence of the Fort name in Tennessee and Cornelia's public status following the Pearl Harbor attack, friends, family, and followers completely filled the cathedral in downtown Nashville. Flowers and messages poured in.

Though asked to speak at the funeral, Nancy Love, who did not feel comfortable speaking in public, declined. However, she did write this endearing note to Cornelia's mother:

> *My feeling about the loss of Cornelia is hard to put into words – I can only say that I miss her terribly, and loved her. She was a rare person. If there can be any comforting thought, it is that she died as she wanted to – in an Army airplane, and in the service of her country.*

Cornelia was buried in Mt. Olivet Cemetery next to her father. BJ and Nancy learned from the inscription on his tombstone that Dr. Fort had died on the very same day as his daughter – March 21 – three years earlier.

The words "Killed in the Service of Her Country" are inscribed on her footstone. Even though the WAFS were civilians, Cornelia Fort is considered to be the first woman pilot in U.S. history to die on active military duty.

Nancy Batson, years later, said that she thought Nancy Love never truly recovered from Cornelia's death. The Women's Auxiliary Ferrying Squadron was Nancy's baby, her creation. She handpicked her pilots. Now she had lost one of her Originals – a friend – and she was devastated.

Nancy Love also wrote a note to Cornelia's instructor, Aubrey Blackburne. Years later Aubrey told Rob Simbeck about the note: "[Nancy Love] said she felt she owed it to me to tell me that the military investigation following the midair collision completely exonerated Cornelia of any blame in any way."

BJ was shaken to the core by Cornelia's death. Losing a good friend who was also under her command, then witnessing the agonizing grief of Cornelia's family, was almost more than she could bear. After the funeral BJ finished her letter home. She wrote:

> *I don't mean to be morbid, but I want to say this. If I should be killed while at my job . . . please just have me cremated and don't have a funeral. . . . I know you would be terribly grieved if I should die, but I am not worried and I have no idea of doing so. But things like this accident do happen and no one is to blame.*
>
> *I have never been happier in my life. I love my work and flying to me is the most wonderful thing I could be doing. The thought of ever getting hurt just never occurs to me. . . .*
>
> *Life must go on despite the loss, and we gals still have a tremendous job to do. We were so terribly saddened by Cornelia's death, but we can't tarry over it. We must go on and fight the harder because she gave her life for it.*

March 1943 was a watershed month for the WAFS. The transitions of Nancy Love and Betty Gillies into pursuit aircraft and Nancy Love and BJ Erickson into flying twin-engine transport planes marked the high point.

Cornelia's devastating death was the rock-bottom low.

Then on March 25, as if things couldn't get worse, they did.

The WAFS of the 3rd Ferrying Group stationed at Romulus, Michigan, were blindsided. The Base Commander put out a directive restricting the WAFS to light trainer aircraft only. Now the women in Romulus could not transition on or fly any high-powered, single-engine or twin-engine aircraft nor were they to fly as copilots on ferrying missions with a male pilot.

The directive stated that women were to be assigned deliveries on alternate days with the male pilots and, if at all possible, were to be sent in a different direction from any male flights. In addition to that, "no mixed flight or crew assignments would be tolerated." This meant women could not "build time" in bigger airplanes by working on transition as copilots to male pilots. They could only work with the men specified as instructors.

Seemingly it was a reaction to Cornelia's accidental meeting with the six male pilots. The men of the military still couldn't figure out how to deal with the women in their presence.

And then came the second blow. A letter from the Air Transport Command went out on March 29, 1943, to all Group Commanders stating that women were not to fly during their menstrual periods – including one day before and two days after. (A real joke considering the vagaries of even the most normal woman's period.)

Was it possible that the military's clueless, all-male command was blaming this tragic plane crash on females' "great unmentionable" – their periods?

Nancy Love was livid!

She had not objected when the Air Transport Command forbade the women to "hitch" rides in other military aircraft cross country following a delivery. The men, of course, were encouraged to do this, but the women had to ride trains and fly on commercial airliners – or find some other slower means of transportation – to get back to base. The primary reason for this was the Army's fear of scandal.

Now, in addition to the insult to the women pilots at Romulus, all the badly needed women pilots were to be grounded for eight or nine days of nonflying time per month because of a normal monthly function of the female body. It was a ridiculous comedy of errors.

Nancy Love had, emphatically, had it! Concerned over the senseless restrictions hurriedly placed on her women ferry pilots in the wake of Cornelia's fatal accident, Nancy went over Colonel Tunner's head directly to General C.R. Smith, a friend from pre-war days. C.R. was now the Air Transport Command's Chief of Staff and General George's second in command.

Nancy knew she could talk to General Smith. She appealed both directives directly to him, even though she risked Colonel Tunner's ire.

Seven WAFS to deliver seven PT-26s: Sis Bernheim, Gertrude Meserve, Dorothy Fulton, Betty Gillies, Helen McGilvery, Teresa James, Nancy Batson. *From the Teresa James collection, author's copy*

Chapter Sixteen

"For Cornelia" Vow the Seven

COLONEL TUNNER HAD SEVEN PT-26s that had to be delivered to the Canadian Royal Air Force near Calgary, Alberta, before Easter in April 1943. It was now the Friday afternoon before Palm Sunday. Knowing the importance of the assignment, Colonel Baker chose his squadron commander at Wilmington, Betty Gillies, to make this important mission happen.

Surprisingly, in spite of the deep sorrow felt by all the WAFS over Cornelia's death, her accident did not bring about resignations nor did it affect the women's desire to ferry airplanes. That went on without a glitch. The women stuck to their ferrying schedules, which speaks highly of the caliber of these professional pilots and to their deep commitment and dedication to their job.

From her Wilmington cadre, Betty selected six experienced pilots and divided them into two "Flights" (sections) for this ferrying trip. The two Flights would fly independently of each other. It was easier for smaller groups to stay together.

Nancy Batson, Sis Bernheim, and Helen McGilvery would fly with Betty in Flight #1. To lead flight #2, Betty assigned Teresa James. Flying with Jamesy would be Gertrude Meserve and Dorothy Fulton.

When they were ready to head off to Canada, Betty Gillies dedicated the long flight to Cornelia. Sis and Helen, who arrived the first of January, barely had time to get to know Cornelia, but Nancy Batson would never forget the fellow Southerner who had so graciously welcomed her to the WAFS.

"For Cornelia," the WAFS agreed.

PT-26s have a cruising speed of about 100 miles per hour. When Betty told her crew where they were going and how long they had to get there, the three stared at her in total disbelief.

"I know, it's more than 2,500 miles, but I promised Colonels Tunner and Baker we'd get them there before Easter," Betty said. Easter was only nine days away.

Nancy Batson let out a long, low whistle. "That doesn't allow for any weather along the route." Betty nodded. "I know." What she didn't tell them was she had great faith in their abilities.

Very early Palm Sunday morning, they were in Hagerstown, Maryland, checking out their aircraft.

"Eeeeyow!" Nancy let out a rebel yell as she climbed into the cockpit of her PT-26. "By golly, we are headin' west in sleek new Army airplanes, and somebody else is paying for the gas."

The other three laughed. They were used to her sudden outbursts of enthusiasm.

They left Hagerstown early, headed west across spring's shades-of-green patchwork quilt of Ohio, Indiana, and Illinois. They ran out of daylight in Joliet, Illinois, but not before they had flown an astounding 697 miles. Nancy noted that, thankfully, the weather was improving over what they had been having in Wilmington. It seemed, to her Alabama blood, like winter lasted forever in Delaware.

Spring definitely was on the way. Besides, PT-26s had enclosed cockpits, so they didn't have to contend with wind in their faces and icicles forming on their runny noses. Tomorrow morning, they would cross the mighty Mississippi.

Nancy Batson recalled the trip in vivid detail:

We were sitting in our cockpits when dawn broke and we were off in a flash, headed due west again. This time our destination was North Platte, Nebraska, a six-hundred-mile flight. We crossed the Mississippi and pretty soon we were looking down on the cornfields of Iowa and later on the wheatfields of Nebraska. It was like I'd never seen corn and wheat fields before. We crossed the Missouri River below Omaha and kept on cruising until we hit North Platte.

We were beginning to enjoy ourselves by then. Here we were, three Easterners and a Southerner, and we were crossing this great big country of ours. This country we were fighting for. And we were so proud of that fact. We were up at four again the next day and, that night, made Great Falls, Montana, a whopping 850-mile flight from North Platte.

When we got there, Betty reminded us – rather proudly, I think – that we had just done it in airplanes that averaged a ground speed of one hundred miles per hour.

"Did you see those mountains!" said Sis, thoroughly taken with the scenery.

Nancy continued with her story:

The next day, up at four again, we flew along those majestic snow-capped Canadian Rockies. What we had seen the previous day was nothing compared to this.

The last leg was a shorty – only 275 miles from Great Falls to a town named DeWinton. We had delivered the planes from Hagerstown in a record four days – and four days before the Easter deadline. Betty had done her job – so had the rest of us. And we had done it well.

We talked a lot on the train ride back. I think we took apart the entire women's flying program and put it together again. Much of the conversation centered around the news that Jackie Cochran's first class of women pilots was destined to

> *swell our ranks early in May. Betty had heard that the class was to graduate April 24 – only two days away. The twenty-three graduates would be divided among the four existing WAFS squadrons.*
>
> *The four of us were back on base by Friday night, April 23 – Good Friday. And do you know what that sweet Colonel Baker did? He gave us all a Commendation — "for our efficient and prompt delivery which included not only flying of the planes but also the paperwork involved in such deliveries, flight logs, gasoline reports, RON messages, etc." I gotta tell you, I'm real proud of that!*

After Betty had signed her four aircraft over to the Canadians, Nancy momentarily caught her eye. "For Cornelia," she said softly, somehow keeping her voice from breaking.

Betty looked steadily at her younger friend and inclined her head in a quiet, heart-breaking nod of acknowledgment.

Yes, as promised, they had done it for Cornelia, their fallen comrade.

On that trip, Betty and her stalwart women pilots proved what Nancy Love already knew – that women made excellent ferry pilots. Nancy could point with pride to this latest accomplishment and tell the military men who oversaw the WAFS that there was a lot more where that came from.

In fact, the women pilots were much more likely than the men to take a plane directly to its delivery point. The men were apt to stop off enroute – even go out of their way – to visit a girlfriend or two. As of April 24, 1943, the WAFS' stock was very high with the entire Ferrying Division – particularly their boss, Colonel Tunner.

And their efforts paid off.

Unbeknownst to those WAFS ferry pilots, just before they left for Canada, General C.R. Smith was in the process of addressing Nancy Love's appeal.

He stated that certain flight limitations were being imposed on women pilots by the Ferrying Division without considering the professional qualifications of the individual pilots; that the ferrying activities of women were being restricted to trainer aircraft only; that women were being prohibited from acting as copilots on ferrying missions; that they were being prohibited from transition training on high-horsepower single-engine or twin-engine aircraft.

General Smith concluded his letter of April 17, 1943, with the following statement: "It is the desire of this Command that all pilots, regardless of sex, be privileged to advance to the extent of their ability in keeping with the progress of aircraft development."

This was a historical breakthrough.

On April 26, Ferrying Division Headquarters issued a new directive. It rescinded the letter of March 29 regarding the WAFS not being allowed to fly during periods of "physical disability" as well as the letter of March 25 forbidding the use of women as copilots with male pilots.

The WAFS would be transitioned on multi-engine and high-power, single-engine aircraft under the same standards of individual experience and ability as any other pilot.

However, still tiptoeing around the morals issue, the directive further stated that normally the WAFS would be given transition on cross-country checkouts by other fully qualified WAFS "when and if available."

Now nothing stood in the way of the WAFS moving up the ladder to qualify in bigger, more powerful aircraft. What General George told Cornelia in the fall of 1942 had become a reality. The WAFS were going to fly the really big ones.

Meanwhile, the investigation into Cornelia's crash exonerated her of any blame in her fatal accident. There was no pilot error on her part.

Thanks to Nancy Love and General C.R. Smith's quick and timely responses, the WAFS program was not only saved it was enhanced.

And, two days before that historical directive supporting the WAFS was announced – April 24, 1943 – the first twenty-three women graduated from the flight training school in Texas. They would be joining the WAFS in the Ferry Command the first week in May. Women pilots would continue to fly for the United States and continue to lend their vital skills to support the war effort.

Cornelia, to whom that critical delivery was dedicated by her fellow WAFS, would have been proud.

Postscript

CORNELIA WROTE THIS thoughtful observation sometime in late fall 1942. Later it became the conclusion to her memorable article *At Twilight's Last Gleaming* that appeared posthumously in *Woman's Home Companion* magazine the summer of 1943:

> *Because there were and are so many disbelievers in women pilots, especially in their place in the army, officials wanted the best possible qualifications to go with the first experimental group. All of us realized what a spot we were on. We had to deliver the goods or else, Or else there wouldn't ever be another chance for women pilots in any part of the service.*
>
> *We have no hopes of replacing men pilots. But we can release a man to combat, to faster ships, to overseas work. Delivering a trainer to Texas may be as important as delivering a bomber to Africa if you take the long view. We are beginning to prove that women can be trusted to deliver airplanes safely and, in the doing, so serve the country – which is our country too.*
>
> *I have yet to have a feeling which approaches satisfaction, that of having signed, sealed, and delivered an airplane for the United States Army. The attitude that most nonfliers have about pilots is distressing and often acutely embarrassing. They chatter about the glamour of flying. Well any pilot can tell you how glamorous it is. We get up in the cold dark in order to get to the airport by daylight.*

We wear heavy cumbersome flying clothes and a thirty-pound parachute. You are either cold or hot. If you are female your lipstick wears off and your hair gets straighter and straighter. You look forward all afternoon to the bath you will have, and the steak. Well, we get the bath but seldom the steak. Sometimes we are too tired and fall wearily in bed.

None of us can put into words why we fly. It is something different for each of us. I can't say exactly why I fly but I know why as I've never known anything in my life.

Cornelia Clark Fort

Epilogue

NASHVILLE, TENNESSEE, did not forget its native daughter Cornelia Clark Fort.

In 1945, two years after her death and with World War II coming to a close, a combined airpark, airport, and air harbor was underway, located near McLean's Bend in the Cumberland River. The airpark was to be named in Cornelia's honor and memory.

Colonel Herbert Fox, then Wing Commander of the Tennessee Civil Air Patrol, told the Nashville newspapers: "The airpark was named 'not only in recognition of Cornelia's service in the field of aviation, but as a tribute to the importance of women in general in this field.'"

Cornelia Fort Airpark was a privately owned, public use airport, elevation 418 feet above sea level with a 3,500-foot-long by 50-foot-wide asphalt surface runway designated 4/22. It runs northeast/southwest.

Engraved on the original historical marker were Cornelia's memorable words from *At Twilight's Last Gleaming.*

> *"I am grateful that my one talent, flying, was useful to my country."*

In 2006, I visited the 141-acre airport on the Cumberland River in East Nashville. I was there attending the Women in Aviation International (WAI) annual conference, just across the river at the Opryland Hotel. I decided I wanted to see – needed to see – the airpark

Photo by the author

named for this amazing woman and fellow Tennessean. My family comes from nearby Murfreesboro.

I did not see the original historical marker. Pictured here is the sign I did see.

It's a good thing I went when I did!

On May 5, 2010, the airport was hit by the horrific floods that struck Nashville that spring. The Cumberland River overflowed its banks, leaving the airport underwater. The flooding rendered the airport unusable. Today the area is part of Shelby Park, a lovely green space northeast of downtown Nashville.

I think Cornelia would have loved that little airport!

The WAFS: "The Originals" Listed in the Order They Were Accepted, 1942-1943

September 5 – December 31, 1942

1. Nancy Love
2. Betty Gillies
3. Cornelia Fort
4. Aline (Pat) Rhonie
5. Helen Mary Clark
6. Adela (Del) Scharr
7. Esther Nelson
8. Teresa James
9. Barbara Poole
10. Helen Richards
11. Barbara Towne
12. Gertrude Meserve
13. Florene Miller
14. Barbara Jane (BJ) Erickson
15. Delphine Bohn
16. Barbara Donahue
17. Evelyn Sharp
18. Phyllis Burchfield

19. Esther Manning
20. Nancy Batson
21. Katherine Rawls Thompson
22. Dorothy Fulton
23. Opal (Betsy) Ferguson
24. Bernice Batten
25. Dorothy Scott

January 1943

26. Helen McGilvery
27. Kathryn (Sis) Bernheim
28. Lenore McElroy

Catherine Slocum completed her training and graduated October 19, but resigned immediately. The family housekeeper had fallen and injured herself. Catherine's husband needed her at home to help with their four children. She never ferried so is not included in the final WAFS count.

Airports Named for Two Other WAFS

TWO MORE OF Nancy Love's original WAFS also lost their lives flying for their country in World War II.

Dorothy Scott, from Oroville, Washington, died December 3, 1943, in a mid-air collision while attending Pursuit School in Palm Springs, California. At fault was the control tower, not the two students flying the two airplanes involved in the collision. Dorothy's instructor and the young pilot of the other plane died as well.

On January 17, 1944, the Oroville town council changed the name of the Oroville Municipal Airport to the Dorothy Scott Municipal Airport. Today it is known as the Dorothy Scott Memorial International Airport (Oroville is only four miles from the Canadian border). More information can be found in my book *Finding Dorothy Scott: Letters of a WASP Pilot*, published in 2016 by the Texas Tech University Press, Lubbock.

Evelyn Sharp, from Ord, Nebraska, died April 3, 1944, ferrying a twin-engine P-38 pursuit aircraft from Long Beach, California, to the docks at Newark, New Jersey. Her left engine quit on takeoff from the New Cumberland, Pennsylvania, Air Depot, and her P-38 crashed in a nearby field.

Evelyn Sharp Field – the Ord, Nebraska, Municipal Airport – was dedicated September 12, 1948. More information can be found in Diane Bartels' book *Sharpie: The Life Story of Evelyn Sharp*, published in 1996 by Dageforde Publishing, Lincoln, Nebraska.

Acknowledgments

I am indebted to and appreciative of:

- My editor Patrice Rhoades-Baum, Sojourn Enterprises, Inc., in appreciation of her sharp eyes and outstanding word sense.
- My marketing manager Mary Walewski, Buy the Book Marketing, who connects me with the wider audience I need to reach to create interest in these stories.
- My book designer Bob Schram, Bookends Design. This is the sixth gorgeous young adult WAFS/WASP book and cover Bob has designed for me.
- The National Aviation Hall of Fame, Dayton, Ohio. In 2019, the NAHF awarded me its Combs Gates Award for my first two WAFS/WASP books for young women readers: *BJ Erickson WASP Pilot* (2018) and *Nancy Love WASP Pilot* (2019). *Cornelia Fort WAFS Pilot* (2023) is the sixth and final book in this series.
- The Fort Family, in particular Lee LaPointe and Dudley Fort, Jr., for their efforts to help me make Cornelia's story the tribute it is meant to be.
- Finally, my thanks to the Sarah Lawrence College Archives and archivist Christina Kasman; to the WASP Archives, Texas

Woman's University, Kimberly Johnson and her marvelous staff; the Nashville, Tennessee, Public Library, Special Collections and staff; and the National Museum of the U.S. Air Force, Dayton, Ohio, my long-time friend Lonna McKinley and her staff.

Bibliography

Published Sources

At Twilight's Last Gleaming: Personal-Experience Narrative of a Member of the WAFS, Karl Detzer, editor, *The Army Reader*, Bobbs-Merrill, 1943

At Twilight's Last Gleaming: Woman's Home Companion magazine, June 1943

Rickman, Sarah Byrn. *The Originals: The Women's Auxiliary Ferrying Squadron of World War II*. Disc Us Books, First Edition, 2001; Braughler Books, Second Edition, 2017

Scharr, Adela Riek. *Sisters in the Sky: Volume One, The WAFS*, The Patrice Press, 1986

Simbeck, Rob. *Daughter of the Air: The Brief Soaring Life of Cornelia Fort*, Atlantic Monthly Press, 1999. Author's note: This book is a significant source of information on Cornelia Fort's life other than my own personal and gathered knowledge of the subject and including my book, *The Originals*.

Warren, Constance – President, Sarah Lawrence College. *A New Design for Women's Education*, published in 1940 by Frederick A. Stokes, Company, New York

Other Sources

Cornelia Fort Collection, WASP Archives, Texas Woman's University Library, Denton, Texas.

Cornelia Fort Collection, Sarah Lawrence College Library and Archives, Bronxville, New York.

Cornelia Fort Collection, the Nashville Tennessee Public Library.

Transcript: An Oral History, Betty Huyler Gillies – Women's Auxiliary Ferrying Squadron. Interviewed by author Rob Simbeck, September 1996, and used with his permission. On file in the WASP Archives, TWU.

Author's Contacts

Author's Personal Interviews (1999) with WAFS Nancy Batson Crews, Teresa James Martin, Gertrude Meserve Tubbs LeValley, and Barbara "BJ" Erickson London.

Author's recent conversations with author Rob Simbeck.

Author's recent conversations with Dudley Fort, Jr., and Lee LaPointe, members of the Fort family.

Books by Sarah Byrn Rickman

- *Cornelia Fort WAFS Pilot: Her Life for Her Country* (2023)
- *Jean Landis WASP Pilot: 2,500 Miles … Long Beach to Newark in a P-51* (2022)
- *Teresa James WAFS Pilot: Gear Up/Gear Down, a P-47 to Newark* (2021)
- *Betty Gillies WAFS Pilot: The Days and Flights of a World War II Squadron Leader* (2000)
- *Nancy Love WASP Pilot* (2019)
- *BJ Erickson WASP Pilot* (2018)
- *Finding Dorothy Scott: Letters of a WASP Pilot* (2016)
- *WASP of the Ferry Command: Women Pilots, Uncommon Deeds* (2016)
- *Flight to Destiny, A WASP Novel* (2014)
- *Nancy Batson Crews: Alabama's First Lady of Flight* (2009)
- *Nancy Love and the WASP Ferry Pilots of World War II* (2008)
- *Flight from Fear, A WASP Novel* (2002)
- *The Originals: The Women's Auxiliary Ferrying Squadron of World War II* (2001)

Also by Sarah Byrn Rickman

- *Six WAFS Up Close and Personal*, a twenty-two-minute documentary film featuring interviews with six Women's Auxiliary Ferrying Squadron pilots: Nancy Batson, Barbara "BJ" Erickson, Teresa James, Gertrude Meserve, Florene Miller, and Barbara Poole, filmed in 1999. Documentary released in 2018.

A Note from Sarah

PLEASE VISIT MY WEBSITE: www.SarahByrnRickman.com. While you're there, click on my Blog link. There, you'll find a virtual library of my blog articles dedicated to WAFS/WASP stories as well as stories of other women flyers of yesterday and today.

Also, click the Subscribe link to receive my biweekly newsletter sent to all my Blog subscribers. Or click Contact to send me a message directly.

And thank you for reading my books!

Sarah and the Aeronca Champ 7-AC (N1798E) that she soloed Friday the 13th of November 2009, and in which she did most of her flying. Photo taken at Red Stewart Airfield outside of Waynesville, Ohio, on November 15, 2010, after Sarah completed her three-leg-cross-country solo. Her route: land first at the nearby local glider field. Takeoff from there and fly to Grimes Field in Urbana, Ohio. Land, taxi back, takeoff, and then return to Red Stewart Airfield where her instructor, Emerson Stewart III, awaited her safe return. It was a warm, cloudless, lovely November day and Grimes Field had a welcoming grass runway on which she could land her taildragger Champ. Sarah passed her check ride and received her Sport Pilot License on July 1, 2011. *Photo from the author's personal collection*

About the Author

CORNELIA FORT WAFS PILOT: *Her Life for Her Country* is Sarah Byrn Rickman's thirteenth book about the women who flew for America in World War II. Her first, *The Originals: The Women's Auxiliary Ferrying Squadron of World War II*, was published in 2001.

In 2017, Sarah switched from writing adult-focused books to writing biographies of these wartime women pilots for the young adult market. Why?

"Today's young women need to hear the incredible stories of these gutsy women who broke the gender barrier in aviation, she says. "The WAFS, later known as the WASP, paved the way for today's women pilots of the U.S. Air Force, Navy, Army, Marines, and Coast Guard – and those flying commercial aircraft as well."

Sarah wanted to write books from the time she was five. After college, she opted first for a career in journalism, was a reporter/columnist at *The Detroit News*, and went on to serve as editor of the twice-weekly *Centerville-Bellbrook Times* in suburban Dayton, Ohio. In addition to writing books, from 2009 to 2019, Sarah served as editor of the *WASP News*, the official newsmagazine for the WASP Archives, located at the Texas Woman's University Library in Denton, Texas.

Sarah realized a lifelong dream in 2011. She earned her Sport Pilot certificate flying an Aeronca Champ – a 1940s-vintage tailwheel aircraft similar to the Cubs and Taylorcraft the WAFS and

WASP learned on, back in the day. She is a member of The Ninety-Nines, Inc., the International Organization for Women Pilots. She also serves as an advisor to the International Women's Air & Space Museum (IWASM) in Cleveland, Ohio, and is active with the National Aviation Hall of Fame in Dayton, Ohio.

To date, Sarah Byrn Rickman has won sixteen book awards.

Purchase her books at www.SarahByrnRickman.com.

Made in the USA
Monee, IL
05 May 2023